The Harrowsmith
PASTA
C O O K B O O K

By the Editors & Readers of Harrowsmith Magazine

Compiled from the private recipe collections of the Editors, Readers,
Contributors and Staff of *Harrowsmith*, Canada's National
Award Winning Magazine of Country Living and Alternatives

CAMDEN HOUSE

Reprinted 1987
Reprinted 1988
Reprinted 1989
Reprinted 1991
Canadian Cataloguing in Publication Data
Main entry under title:
The Harrowsmith pasta cookbook
Includes index.
ISBN 0-920656-15-3
I. Cookery (Macaroni). I. Cross, Pamela.
II. Harrowsmith.
TX809.M17H37 1984   641.8'22   C84-099417-6

Trade distribution by Firefly Books, Toronto

Printed in Canada by
Friesen Printers, Altona, Manitoba, for

Camden House Publishing
(a division of Telemedia Publishing Inc.)
7 Queen Victoria Road
Camden East, Ontario
K0K 1J0

Cover illustration by Roger Hill

The Harrowsmith
PASTA
COOKBOOK

Editor
Pamela Cross

Associate Editor
Alice Pitt

Photography
Ernie Sparks

Food Design
Mariella Morrin

Copy Editors
Charlotte DuChene, David Archibald

Graphic Design
Philip Wood

Photography Credits
PHOTOGRAPHIC PROPERTIES COURTESY OF:
KITCHEN CARGO, 57 BROCK ST., KINGSTON, ONTARIO
McCALLUM'S CHINA AND GIFTS LTD., 79 BROCK ST., KINGSTON, ONTARIO
BOUTIQUE LISETTE, 300 KING ST. E., KINGSTON, ONTARIO
Special Assistance:
NICLA SIVILOTTI, GLENN E. ANGLIN, MIRELLA GUIDI, CHARLES PANET

CONTENTS

INTRODUCTION

FACE TO FACE WITH PASTA FOR THE FIRST TIME, all too many of us found ourselves confronted by a childhood plateful of sodden little letters, bloated almost beyond recognition and drowning in a gelatinous, ketchup-like sauce laced with sugar. Entombed in a tin for months, if not longer, these distended bits of alphabetical noodle may have thrilled our 6-year-old palates, but they can hardly have fostered the beginning of a lifelong love and respect for pasta proper.

Consider the great composer Gioacchino Rossini, whose young taste buds were never exposed to the starchy sensations of Alphagetti, Scarios or Zoodles and who grew up to become as passionate and eloquent a fan of pasta cookery as history has known. Once, finding himself stranded in Paris in 1859, far from his native Italy and its cottage pasta makers, Rossini wrote a friend bemoaning the dire lack of good, authentic pasta in France and signed himself "Rossini Senzamaccheroni" – Rossini Without Macaroni. While remembered by most for his operas, Rossini is also known to some as a great innovator in the kitchen. In one case, for example, he had a special syringe constructed of silver and ivory with which he injected large tubular noodles with a rich concoction of pâté de foie gras, beef marrow and truffles. Clearly unintimidated by the French culinary hauteur that surrounded him, Rossini wrote: "You need intelligence to cook, mix and serve pasta."

This proud perception is clearly beginning to be shared by growing numbers of North Americans who are discovering in pasta an ingredient with almost limitless creative possibilities – an intelligent choice for the cook who is always on the alert for fresh ideas and different taste sensations.

One of the few foods that can be as elegant as it is economical, pasta is far more than simply spaghetti and meatballs or noodles in cheese sauce. It can form any part of a meal – from appetizers through soups and desserts – and it comes in a bewildering and exciting array of shapes and textures from cultures throughout the world. Crispy Jao Tze from China, Korean acorn-starch noodles (*Mo mil kook so*), Middle Eastern couscous, Jewish kreplach, German "little sparrow" dumplings called spaetzle, eastern European perogi, North American egg flakes and Amish potpie – all are pasta. As variable as it is versatile, pasta can be as simple as a platter of fresh-made fettuccine tossed lightly with olive oil and a hint of garlic or as sumptuous as Arrezzo Lasagne or Penne with Crab and Shrimp.

Although late in coming to appreciate pasta, we North Americans cannot help but marvel at a food that is both delicious and possessed of many nutritionally attractive qualities. Low in sodium and fat, pasta is high in the complex carbohydrates that are so sadly lacking in the modern ultra-high-protein diet. The substitution of meat and fats with foods such as pasta is not only part of the contemporary regimen of Olympic athletes and marathon runners but is also a fast-growing trend among those conscious of their intestinal and cardiovascular health.

Recent medical surveys of communities in southern Italy, where pasta plays a significant nutritional role — 80 percent of families there serve it twice a day — demonstrated lower rates of both heart disease and cancer. Likewise, a study of an Italian-American ethnic neighbourhood that had adhered to the Old World staples of pasta and wine showed almost no signs of heart disease in individuals under 40 and a 25 percent lower incidence of cardiovascular problems than the general population.

While we eat an average of about 10 pounds of pasta per capita, Italians consume something on the order of 70 pounds for every man, woman and child each year. Our grudging acceptance of pasta is due, in part, to the firmly entrenched notion that noodles and spaghetti and their ilk are notoriously fattening. In fact, ounce for ounce, pasta itself has less calories than lean turkey meat, or a low 210 calories for a four-ounce serving. Even fully dressed with sauce, a normal adult portion of spaghetti can be served with but a modest 400 to 500 calories. While providing essential energy mobilizers in the form of complex carbohydrates, pasta has virtually none of the fats and simple sugars that saturate our diet. By volume, pasta has less calories than either rice or potatoes, while providing important nutrients and satisfying the demands of light and hearty appetites alike.

ENIGMATIC ORIGINS

If you were to travel 30 miles north of Rome to a certain Etruscan tomb famous for its bas-relief sculptures, you would find two magnificent columns that record the everyday kitchen utensils of the 4th century B.C. One is especially noteworthy for its portrayal of a readily identifiable rolling-table, pitcher, ladle, rolling pin, sack of flour, knife and cutting wheel — the basic tools of pasta making that remain little changed today.

Just where pasta originated is a hotly debated subject, partly confused by the apocryphal tale of Marco Polo bringing the idea of noodle making back from China in 1295. In fact, a now well-known notarized will, written in 1279, records a Genoese sailor's bequest of a *bariscella piena de macaroni* — a small basket of macaroni.

Although popularly thought of as an Italian specialty, pasta and its history are ill contained by national borders, primarily because of the simplicity of its formula — ground grain or flour and water. (Pasta means paste in Italian.) Western pasta is usually made with wheat flour and water, while other cultures use mung-bean starch, soya flour, potato starch, buckwheat, rice and acorns. Most food historians agree that the invention of pasta must have occurred in various places and at different times, as early agricultural peoples discovered that their wild grain could be made into a paste, dried and later reconstituted — months or even years later — by cooking or soaking in water. The benefits of such a storable, transportable staple must have been immediately clear to nomadic tribes and to those subsisting on prehistoric crops.

By the Middle Ages, many parts of the world included words for pasta in their vocabularies. English "noodles," French *nouilles* and German *nudeln* all derive from the Latin word *nodellus*, meaning knot. The Italian word spaghetti comes from *spago*, meaning string, and not from the name of one of Polo's sailors, as the American trade magazine *The Macaroni Journal* fancifully reported in 1929.

The term macaroni itself dates from the Middle Ages and may have come from the Sicilian *macco*, meaning flour and water paste, or from the Greek *makac*, meaning food of the blessed, or *makar*, which means divinely holy or blessed antidote to all ills. Macaroni now refers to eggless pasta of the tubular type, a common form in southern Italy. In fact, travellers to Naples in the early years of this century came home with exuberant tales of the *maccheronaros* — macaroni sellers — found on busy street corners, hawking dried pasta as well as cooked and dressed dishes. Until the making of noodles moved into centralized factories, curtains of drying pasta hung from fences and in dooryards everywhere in Naples, which even in mediaeval times had been the centre of a powerful pasta-making guild.

There is evidence that pasta was being manufactured in many shapes by the 1400s — today, at least 325 different pastas are known — and during the 18th century, all of Europe was enjoying Italian history and culture. Their introduction came, in part, from young aristocrats who had the means to travel and a penchant for lavishing praise on their homeland. Their less-well-to-do contemporaries soon tired of the Italian manners and their poems in praise of pasta and caustically dubbed these unofficial ambassadors "macaronis."

Nonetheless, the world of food remains indebted to Italy for the advancement of pasta cookery, and many connoisseurs contend that the best Western commercial pasta still comes from Italy, perhaps unaware that the flour is imported from Canada and the United States. The role of North

American wheat in the development of fine pasta owes a great deal to an American agronomist named Mark Carleton, who travelled to Russia in 1898 in search of a disease-resistant variety to replace the rust-ravaged North American wheats. What he brought back was kubanka, a grain resistant both to rust blight and to drought, and this wheat quickly became established in North Dakota and Manitoba. Now known as durum wheat, it yields an exceptionally hard kernel high in gluten from which the epitome of pasta ingredients – semolina – is milled. Italian law now dictates that dried commercial pastas must be made only with pure durum wheat flour.

FATTA EN CASA

One participant in the editing of this book contends that he can, without undue haste or stress, start with a cold kitchen and, 20 minutes later, place a steaming platter of homemade egg-fettuccine noodles on the family dinner table – aided only by a Cuisinart pasta maker and assisted by his 7-year-old daughter.

Although commercial dried pastas are among the more wholesome manufactured goods on the modern supermarket shelf, fresh, homemade pasta is of another dimension, in terms of flavour and texture. It can be made with ease by even the most inexperienced cook and, in its most basic forms, requires nothing not normally found in most home kitchens. Once one has tasted good, fresh pasta, one is committed to a lifetime of making it.

All that is needed to make flat noodles is a wooden spoon, a mixing bowl and a rolling pin. A flat counter is also required, or a wooden board three or four feet square. (Essential items in many Italian kitchens are a family pasta board – which is never washed but only scraped and wiped clean – and an eight-quart boiling pot.) Following the directions in the next chapter, basic homemade pasta – *pasta fatta en casa* – is readily within reach.

To make macaroni, rigatoni, zite and other tubular noodles, one must have an electric machine to accomplish the extrusion process, and there is no doubt that kitchen counter pasta makers have proved very popular with many cooks. They are, however, expensive to purchase, and a good intermediate step is the familiar chromed hand-operated pasta machine, which greatly eases the steps of rolling and cutting the dough for flat noodles. These manual pasta makers are virtually indestructible, provided they are used with reasonable care. Do not overload the machine with too much dough. Turn the rollers at moderate speed, and put the dough through each setting twice (see photographs in following chapter). Clean with a stiff brush and a dry cloth, never using water.

COOKING & HOVERING

On a recent evening in Toronto, and in the line of dedicated research, we visited a newly opened restaurant complex featuring "Canada's finest" Italian cooking under the supervision of one of the country's leading gourmet restaurateurs. When the pasta course arrived, we were dismayed to be greeted by a limp mass of vermicelli, suffocating in its own glue.

Someone, clearly, had forgotten the first rule of serving pasta: It must not, cannot, be overcooked. To do so shows not so much a lack of skill, but a lack of care, for cooking pasta involves but a few tricks:

• Use a generous amount of water — four to five quarts per pound of pasta — to allow even cooking and to prevent sticking. Bring the water to a rumbling boil before adding the pasta.

• Just prior to introducing the pasta, you may wish to add a tablespoon each of vegetable oil and salt. Some cooks are convinced that the oil helps retard foaming and keeps the individual pieces of pasta separate. The salt, preferably granular and noniodized, adds flavour and raises the boiling point of water, to help seal in the starches.

• Do not attempt to cook more than two pounds of pasta per batch.

• Add pasta all at once, and maintain a careful vigilance until the meal is on the table. Fresh pasta will cook in just a minute or two and must be watched constantly.

• Dried pasta may take up to 15 or 20 minutes and must be watched closely as it nears doneness. Perfect pasta is tender and firm, but never raw or hard at the core or with any trace of a floury taste. It must never be mushy. When testing, lift a single strand out of the water and bite carefully. Properly cooked, pasta is *al dente* — it can be felt by the teeth — and never sticky. The key to all of this is hovering — never forgetting that the pasta must be tested throughout its cooking process. It is hardly tedious work, and the results tell the difference between a good cook and one who is careless or ill informed.

• Once done, pasta should be drained immediately in a metal colander. Some devotees wash immediately with hot water to rinse away any starch, while others drain quickly and toss lightly with butter or oil to keep the individual strands well separated. Serve immediately.

• If the pasta is to be baked, as in lasagne or cannelloni, undercook it slightly to allow for the further cooking time in the oven. Fresh pasta, in fact, need not be boiled at all, but simply added to the casserole and baked.

THE GRACEFUL FORK

A final word is necessary on the subject of eating pasta, the rules for which are as scrambled and confused in the public mind as a dropped pot of cappellini. While the lumber-camp style is to attack spaghetti with knife, fork and spoon, cutting the unruly lengths down to size whenever one wishes, this is to be avoided. (Hexes upon the cook who breaks spaghetti strands before cooking.)

Followers of Emily Post will know that one must use a spoon and fork, twirling the strands around the fork while using the spoon's face as a back-stop.

The purist Italian manners are explicit on this, however: one uses only his or her fork. Insert the tines briskly into the mass of pasta, twirl a number of strands around the fork (using the curve of the plate to steady the fork), and lift to the mouth. If one or two strands trail slightly loose, a common phenomenon with fresh spaghetti, consider this almost unavoidable. Be decorous, but remember, this is pasta, unlike any other food. Savour it.

 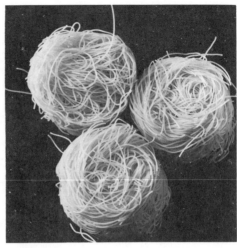

*The noodles pictured on these two pages are all flat noodles and can be made by hand. **Above**, are two varieties of fine egg noodles, available commercially either loose or in birds' nests. An even finer noodle called vermicelli is used often in Chinese cooking.*

*Spaghettini, **above left**, is the finest of the traditional Italian spaghettis. **Above right** is pictured spinach spaghetti that has been made by hand and hung on a rack to dry.*

Classic Pastas

 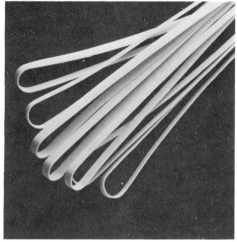

Linguine, **above left**, is another flat noodle but is broader than spaghetti. It is commercially available in a number of flavours — egg, whole wheat and spinach, to mention a few. Fettuccine, **top right**, is slightly broader than linguine.

Broader yet are fettucce, **above left**, and egg noodles such as those pictured **above right**.

Pictured on these two pages are tubular macaronis. These are produced by extrusion, so cannot be made by a hand-operated machine. There are, however, home-sized electric machines for producing fresh tubular pastas. Once again, there are a number of sizes of long tubular noodles. **Above left** *is the narrow bucatine,* and **above right,** *the somewhat broader perciatelli.*

Above left, *zite, and* **above right**, *zitone, can both be served successfully with a rich, creamy cheese sauce.*

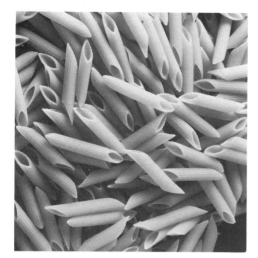 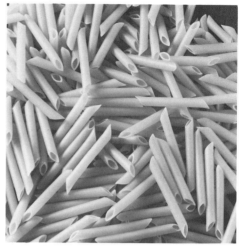

Tubular macaronis can also be cut into varying lengths. Penne rigate, **above left**, *is ribbed as well. Pennine,* **above right**, *is a finer, smooth-surfaced version of penne.*

Cannaroni lisci, **above left**, *is basically a large elbow macaroni. Rigatoni,* **above right**, *is a yet-again larger macaroni.*

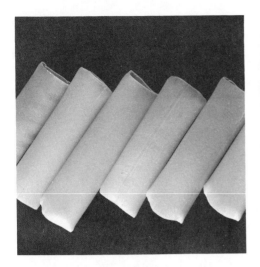 

Cannelloni, **above left**, *and manicotti,* **above right**, *although tubular, can both be made by hand. Simply roll out the dough to the desired thinness, place filling in centre, and roll into tube, sealing edge. Manicotti is a slightly thicker, bigger tube than cannelloni.*

Lasagne, **above left**, *is also easily made by hand — to get the fluted edge, cut with a pizza cutter. Rotini,* **above right**, *is a spiral pasta which is only available commercially.*

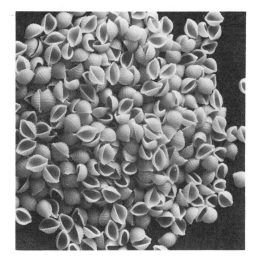 

Pictured on this page are a number of pastas that cannot be produced at home. All are best served with a fairly heavy sauce that can work its way into the openings of the noodles. Shell noodles are available in a variety of sizes, from small, **above left**, *to jumbo,* **above right.**

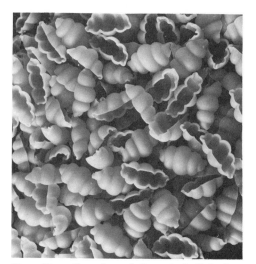 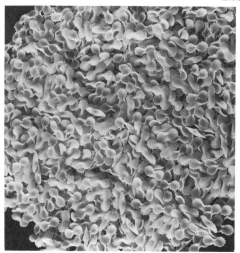

Gnocchi noodles, **above left**, *and tripolini,* **above right**, *are two other varieties.*

Pictured on this page are three filled pastas and gnocchi. These need only to be boiled, topped with tomato sauce and cheese, and served. All can be bought easily in the frozen-food section of the grocery store but can also be made at home. The tortellini, **above left**, is filled with meat, and the ravioli, **above right**, with cheese.

 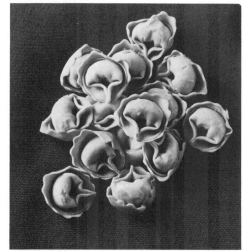

The capletts, **above right**, are filled with spinach and cheese. The gnocchi is pictured **above left.**

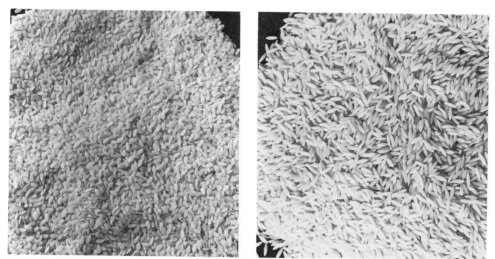

Two pastas which resemble grains in their appearance are semi di mellone, **top left**, *and orzo,* **top right**. *Both are, however, true pastas in ingredients, cooking methods and taste.*

HOW-TO

You have to know the rules before you can break them

PASTA HOW-TO

THERE ARE ALMOST LIMITLESS WAYS TO MAKE PASTA. MANY KINDS OF flour can be used, and vegetables, herbs and even fruit rind can be added to change colour, texture and flavour. The dough can be mixed by hand or food processor, rolled out and cut manually or by using one of a variety of pasta makers; there are even machines that do the whole operation from beginning to end. We provide here a few basic recipes for dough, but as long as care is taken so that a workable dough results, the only limit is the cook's own imagination. Here, too, are step-by-step photographs, with instructions for making pasta by hand and by using a food processor and pasta machine.

Fresh pasta can be used immediately, in which case it needs to be cooked for only 1 or 2 minutes in rapidly boiling water to which a teaspoon of oil has been added. This prevents the pasta from sticking together. The noodles should be dropped into the water in small handfuls and stirred gently to eliminate clumping.

If it is to be stored, it should be hung until it is completely dry — 12 hours. It should then be tightly bagged and stored in a cool place. Homemade pasta can be frozen as well. This pasta will still cook much more quickly than will commercial pasta. The dough can be made up and kept for several hours if well wrapped to prevent it from drying out.

Most hand-operated pasta machines come with a variety of cutters for flat noodles. Of course, it is a simple matter to cut noodles by hand, using a sharp knife, into whatever shape and size is desired. In order to make any of the tubular noodles (such as macaroni, zite, et cetera), it is necessary to have a machine that operates on the extrusion principle — these are electric rather than manual and are generally considerably more expensive.

Wooden pasta dryers can be purchased relatively inexpensively, but a broom handle propped between two chairs can be used with equal success.

BASIC PASTA DOUGH

2 cups flour
3 eggs
2 tsp. oil
2 Tbsp. water

To make dough by hand, mound flour on work surface, and make a well in the centre. Combine eggs, oil and water, and pour into well. Mix all together, using a fork at first and then working by hand. Knead dough for 5 to 8 minutes, or until it is smooth and elastic. Cover and let stand for 10 minutes.

If using a food processor, place all ingredients in machine and process until a ball forms. Knead for 2 to 4 minutes or until smooth and elastic. Cover and let stand for 2 minutes.

In either case, if dough is too wet, add flour; if too dry, add an egg.

To roll pasta by hand, divide dough into thirds, and roll on floured board until desired thinness. This is hard work and will take some time and muscle power. Cut as desired.

If using a pasta machine, divide dough into thirds, and begin with rollers at first setting, rolling twice through each setting, until desired thinness is attained. Cut by machine or by hand.

PASTA VARIATIONS

Vegetable: Almost any cooked, puréed vegetables can be used. For green pasta, use spinach, broccoli or peas. Tomatoes or carrots result in an orange noodle. For a bright red colour, use beets. Cook vegetables until tender, then purée, leaving vegetables coarse enough that the pasta will have texture as well as flavour.

For the above amount of pasta, use ½ cup cooked, puréed vegetables and one less egg. Prepare dough as directed above.

Herbs: Wash, dry and chop finely 4 Tbsp. of herb desired (or a combination) — parsley, sage, basil, thyme and tarragon are a few possibilities. Mix with flour before adding remaining ingredients. For a beautiful yellow dough, dissolve a small amount of saffron in 2 Tbsp. boiling water, and use in place of the cold water.

Other Flours: To make whole wheat pasta, use 1½ cups whole wheat flour and ½ cup unbleached white flour. Other flour possibilities include semolina, buckwheat and triticale.

1

2

3

4

Making pasta by hand

Place 2 cups flour in bowl, (1), or on work surface, mounding it up. Add 2 teaspoons oil, (2), then 3 eggs, (3), then 2 tablespoons water, (4). Alternatively, the oil, eggs and water can be mixed together and added all at once. Mix dough with wooden spoon, (5), until it holds together, then work by hand, (6).

5

6

7

8

9

Continue working dough, (7), until it forms a ball, (8). Knead, (9), for 5 to 8 minutes, or until smooth and elastic. Additional flour may be worked in if necessary. Let dough sit, covered, for 10 minutes.

10

11

12

Roll dough out, (10), dusting with flour to keep rolling pin from sticking, until it is paper thin, (11). Trim off any really uneven pieces, then gently roll up from both sides, meeting in the middle, (12).

13

14

Cut dough into desired width for noodles, (13), using a sharp knife and pressing down as gently as possible. Carefully unfold noodles, (14), and dry or cook as needed.

Place 2 cups flour, (1), 2 eggs, 2 teaspoons oil and 2 tablespoons water, (2), and ½ cup cooked, puréed spinach, (3), in bowl of food processor. Because of the liquid in the spinach, 1 less egg is used than in the basic pasta recipe.

Making spinach pasta
in a food processor

4

5

6

Place lid on food processor and whir for a few seconds, (4). Check the dough, (5), and once it holds together when pressed between the fingers, place it on work surface, (6).

7

8

9

Work dough by hand, (7), kneading until it forms a smooth elastic dough, (8). Put through pasta machine at first setting, (9). Put through this setting a second time.

10

11

12

Continue pressing through pasta machine, (10) and (11), twice at each setting, until desired thinness is reached. For fettuccine, the fifth setting is usually adequate, for spaghetti, the sixth. The noodles can be cut according to preference and availability of attachments. Here, (12), they are being cut into fettuccine.

13

14

Spaghetti, (13), can also be cut with most standard hand-operated pasta machines. If dough tends to stick in rollers or cutters, sprinkle it liberally with flour. Pasta can be hung to dry on a wooden pasta dryer, (14), or on a broomstick placed between 2 chairs.

Roll dough out to thinnest setting on a pasta machine, or to paper thinness by hand. Cut into rectangles that are approximately 4 inches wide, (1), then cut into squares, (2). Place 1 to 2 tablespoons of filling in centre of square, forming it into a tube, (3).

Making cannelloni

Roll noodle up, working away from you, (4) and (5), sealing edge with water if necessary. Place edge-side down in greased casserole dish. Continue with remaining noodles.

1   2

Roll dough out and cut as for cannelloni (pages 34-35). Place 1 to 2 teaspoons of filling in centre of wrapper, (1). Wet edges of wrapper with water, (2).

Making won tons

3

4

Fold won ton in half, pressing edges together firmly to seal well, (3). Take both short edges and turn them in and under to shape the won ton, (4).

1

2

3

Roll dough as thin as possible by hand, or to thinnest setting of pasta machine. Cut into circles with a 2½"-3" diameter, (1). Place 1 teaspoon of filling in centre of circle, (2). Fold dough over filling to form a half-moon, sealing edges well. Take 2 corners of half-moon and pinch together to form tortellini, (3).

Making tortellini

1

2

Shape dough into solid tube 1 inch in diameter on work surface, (1). Cut crosswise into 1-inch pieces, (2). Press flat sides with a fork, (3), then cook in boiling water.

3

Making gnocchi

APPETIZERS

An omen of good things to come

ANTIPASTO

THIS IS NOT A PASTA RECIPE BUT IS A TRADITIONAL FIRST COURSE IN AN Italian meal (antipasto means "before pasta"). Serve with crackers, or make a more elaborate appetizer by adding sliced cheeses, salami, bread sticks and other pickles.

1 cup olive oil
4 cups sliced mushrooms
9 cups Spicy Tomato Sauce, page 96
1 large head cauliflower, cut into bite-sized pieces
2 large green peppers, cut into bite-sized pieces
1 large red pepper, cut into bite-sized pieces
5 cups green beans, cut into ¼-inch lengths, cooked
3 6½-oz. cans tuna
3 6½-oz. cans shrimp
3 15-oz. cans stuffed green olives
3 15-oz. cans pitted black olives
2 large jars pickled onions
Tabasco sauce
Lemon juice
Salt & pepper

Heat 3 Tbsp. oil, and sauté mushrooms briefly.

In heavy pot, mix remaining oil with 8 cups Spicy Tomato Sauce, cauliflower, green and red peppers, beans and mushrooms. Bring to a boil, reduce heat to low, and cook for 10 minutes.

Drain and rinse tuna and shrimp. Add to tomato-vegetable mixture. If mixture seems too thick, add reserved Spicy Tomato Sauce. Add olives and onions, then Tabasco sauce, lemon juice and salt and pepper to taste.

Pack into sterilized 8-oz. jars, and process in boiling water bath for 15 minutes. Once opened, keep refrigerated and use quickly.

Makes 8 to 10 quarts.

— *Charlie & Mary Zoretich*
Celista, British Columbia

THE FOLLOWING RECIPES ARE ALL, BASICALLY, VARIATIONS ON THE THEME of deep-fried stuffed pasta. They originate in many different countries — jao-tze are from northern China, egg rolls and won tons from central China, perogies from the Ukraine and samosas from India.

PEROGIES

THESE DUMPLINGS CAN BE FILLED WITH POTATOES AND CHEESE OR cabbage. They are then cooked until golden brown, but still soft, unlike egg rolls, samosas and won tons, which are deep-fried until crisp.

Dough
3 cups flour
1 tsp. salt
1 tsp. oil
1 egg, beaten

Potato Filling
3 potatoes, peeled & cooked
Milk
Butter
¾ cup grated Cheddar cheese
Salt & pepper

Cabbage Filling
2 Tbsp. oil
1 onion, chopped
2 cups sauerkraut
1 Tbsp. brown sugar
Pepper
1 cup butter

For dough, combine flour, salt and oil. Add egg and enough water to make a smooth, soft ball of dough — about 1 cup. Knead for 3 to 5 minutes, then let rest, covered, for 30 minutes.

To make potato filling, mash the potatoes with enough milk and butter to make a smooth but stiff purée. Mix in cheese while potatoes are still hot. Season with salt and pepper.

For cabbage filling, heat oil and sauté onion until tender. Rinse sauerkraut in cold water and drain well. Add to onion with sugar and pepper. Fry, turning cabbage occasionally, until it is lightly browned. Cool.

Divide ball of dough in half. Roll out to ⅛-inch thickness, then cut into 3-inch squares.

Place a heaping teaspoonful of either filling in each square, fold dough over to form a triangle, and pinch edges with fingers to seal.

Melt butter, then cook perogies until heated through and golden brown. Serve with sour cream.

Serves 4.

— Ann Kostendt
St. Thomas, Ontario

SAMOSAS

THE FILLINGS FOR SAMOSAS ARE BASED ON GROUND MEAT OR POTATOES and seasoned with a combination of curry spices. The samosas should be fried until the wrappers are very crispy.

1 recipe Basic Pasta Dough, page 23

Meat Filling
¾ lb. ground pork
2 green onions, chopped
2 cloves garlic, crushed
1 tsp. chopped ginger
2 tsp. cumin
¾ tsp. coriander
½ tsp. turmeric
½ tsp. dried red pepper
Salt & pepper

Potato Filling
4 cups cubed, cooked potatoes
1½ cups peas
2 tsp. curry
Salt & pepper

2 eggs, beaten
4 cups oil

Prepare dough, roll out to 1/16-inch thickness by hand or by using pasta machine. Cut into 5-inch squares.

For meat filling, brown pork, onions, garlic and ginger. When meat has lost its pinkness, stir in spices and cook for a few more minutes. Remove from heat and drain off fat.

Combine potatoes, peas, curry and salt and pepper.

Place 2 or 3 tablespoons of either filling in the centre of each samosa wrapper. Fold wrapper in half, sealing well with beaten egg.

Heat oil to 375 degrees F and cook samosas until golden brown and crispy. Drain on paper towelling.

Serves 6.

EGG ROLLS

FILLED WITH VEGETABLES WITH A MILDLY GINGERY FLAVOUR, EGG rolls, like samosas and won tons, are deep-fried until crispy.

½ recipe Basic Pasta Dough, page 23
Filling
½ lb. bean sprouts
¼ cup diced mushrooms
2 cups shredded cabbage
½ cup chopped water chestnuts
½ cup chopped bamboo shoots
2 green onions, finely chopped
1 tsp. sherry
1 tsp. tamari sauce
1 tsp. chopped ginger
1 clove garlic, crushed

1 egg, beaten
4 cups oil

Prepare pasta dough, and roll out to 1/16-inch thickness by hand or by using pasta machine. Cut into 6-inch squares and keep covered with a damp cloth.

Combine remaining ingredients for filling. Mix well.

To assemble, spoon 2 Tbsp. of filling onto lower corner of wrapper in a sausage shape. Fold lower corner over filling until just covered. Roll it over once again.

Moisten left and right corners of triangle with egg, fold them over, and press down firmly to seal. The egg roll will look like an envelope with its flap up. Moisten flap with egg, and turn it down over the envelope. Seal firmly.

Heat oil in wok to 375 degrees F. Cook egg rolls until crisp and golden brown. Drain on paper towelling.

Serves 6.

WON TONS

THE FILLINGS FOR WON TONS CAN BE VARIED TO SUIT PERSONAL
preference. Given here is a basic meat stuffing and a vegetarian filling.
Both fillings as well as the wrappers can be frozen. Each filling recipe
provided below will fill about half the number of wrappers given by the
dough.

1 recipe Basic Pasta Dough, page 23

Meat Filling
½ lb. ground pork
½ lb. chopped shrimp
½ cup chopped cooked spinach
1 egg, beaten
1 Tbsp. Chinese wine
2 Tbsp. tamari sauce
1 Tbsp. cornstarch
Salt & pepper

Vegetarian Filling
½ cup chopped water chestnuts
½ cup chopped watercress
½ cup bean sprouts
½ cup chopped Chinese cabbage
2 Tbsp. tamari sauce
1 tsp. chopped ginger root
1 clove garlic, crushed

4 cups oil

Prepare dough, cover, and set aside.

Combine all ingredients for meat filling, mix well by hand, and set aside.
For vegetarian filling, mix all ingredients together with a wooden spoon.

Roll dough to 1/16-inch thickness, or put through a pasta machine to
thinnest setting. Cut into 3-inch squares. Keep these covered with a damp
towel to prevent drying.

Place a teaspoon of filling on each square and then form into won tons as
explained and illustrated on page 36-37.

Heat oil to 375 degrees F. Fry won tons, a few at a time, until crispy and
golden brown. Drain well, and serve.

Makes approximately 4 dozen won tons.

FRIED JAO-TZE

ORIGINATING IN NORTHERN CHINA, THESE ARE ESSENTIALLY FRIED dumplings. They may also be steamed or boiled. When fried, they serve as delicious finger food. A variety of dips can be offered as accompaniment – honey mustard sauce, soya sauce with ginger and vinegar, sweet and sour sauce and so on.

Dough
1½ cups unbleached flour
8 Tbsp. water

Filling
6 Chinese mushrooms
⅓ lb. ground pork
½ cup diced bamboo shoots
⅓ cup chopped shrimp
1½ Tbsp. Chinese sherry
1½ Tbsp. tamari sauce
1 Tbsp. cornstarch
Salt
½ egg, beaten

⅓ cup oil

To make dough, place flour in bowl and add water, mixing by hand until well blended. Knead, cover and let stand for 45 minutes.

For filling, cover mushrooms with boiling water. Let stand for 20 minutes, drain, then squeeze to extract most of the moisture. Cut off stems and discard, then chop mushrooms.

Combine pork, bamboo shoots, mushrooms, shrimp, sherry, tamari sauce, cornstarch, salt and egg and mix well. Refrigerate for several hours, or place in freezer for a few minutes.

Place dough on lightly floured board. Knead until smooth and elastic – about 5 minutes. Stretch into sausage shape, then pull off 25 to 30 equal-sized pieces. Roll into balls, then flatten and roll into 3-inch circles. Cover circles as you make them to prevent drying.

Place 2 teaspoons filling in centre of each circle. Bring edges of dough up, and pinch together firmly in the centre, forming a crescent. Use a little water to seal, and leave each end open. Make a pleat in one end, then gather up the rest of the dough on the end, making 3 or 4 pleats facing the centre of the crescent. Repeat at other end. Once again, keep finished crescents covered.

Heat oil. Cook dumplings until golden brown on the bottom – about 2 minutes. Pour 1 cup water all around the dumplings. Cover pot as tightly as possible, and cook over high heat until water almost boils away – 5 minutes – then turn heat to low. After 5 more minutes, turn heat to high long enough to brown dumplings well on bottom. Serve bottom side up.

Makes 25 to 30 dumplings, which will serve 6 as an appetizer.

SOUPS

*There's love to warm your weary heart
and soup to warm your bones*

CAPPELLETTINI IN BRODO

CAPPELLETTINI MEANS LITTLE HATS IN ITALIAN, AND BRODO MEANS broth. This dish is so named because the filled pasta triangles resemble the three-cornered hats popular at the time of Napoleon I. They are also known as "the Navel of Venus."

Pasta
1 egg
1 egg yolk
1 cup flour
1 tsp. salt
1 Tbsp. water

Filling
2 chicken breasts, boned
2 green onions
2 Tbsp. oil
Fresh thyme, oregano, sage & parsley
Garlic powder
1 egg yolk
Parmesan cheese
Salt & pepper
Bread crumbs
20 cups rich chicken broth

Make pasta dough as on page 23. Cover and set aside.

Sauté chicken breasts and onions in oil until chicken is cooked through but not browned.

Blend herbs to taste in food processor in order given, blending each before adding the next. Blend in garlic powder, egg yolk, 2 Tbsp. Parmesan cheese, the cooked chicken breasts, and salt and pepper to taste. Add bread crumbs if needed to make a pasta-like consistency.

Roll a large tablespoon of this mixture into a pencil-thick coil. Put pasta through pasta machine to thinnest setting, or roll out until paper thin. Cut pasta into 1-inch squares.

Pinch off a small piece of the chicken coil, and place in the middle of the pasta square. Press the 2 opposite corners of the pasta firmly together, making a triangle and sealing the chicken inside. Wrapping the triangle around 1 finger, press the smallest corners together and turn down the middle point of the triangle. Repeat until all the pasta and filling have been used.

Poach cappellettini in broth for 13 to 15 minutes. Serve garnished with parsley and Parmesan cheese.

Serves 8 to 10.

— Mirella Guidi
Kingston, Ontario

CHINESE MUSHROOM SOUP

1 oz. black mushrooms
4 cups vegetable stock
3 Tbsp. oil
1 large onion, sliced
2 cloves garlic, crushed
½ lb. mushrooms, sliced
3 Tbsp. flour
¼ cup tamari sauce
½ cup orzo
Chopped parsley
Chopped green onion
Salt & pepper

Wash black mushrooms carefully. Bring stock to a boil, add mushrooms, and simmer for 30 minutes.

Remove mushrooms from stock to cool, and reserve stock. Slice mushroom caps.

Heat oil. Sauté onion, garlic, mushrooms and black mushrooms. Stir in flour and tamari sauce, return stock to pot, and simmer for 30 minutes. Add orzo and cook for 10 more minutes. Add parsley, green onion and salt and pepper to taste.

Serves 4.

CHICKEN SEASHELL SOUP

1 stewing hen
½ cup chopped celery
½ small onion, chopped
1 bay leaf
Nutmeg
Salt & pepper
1½ cups chopped green onions
5 carrots, chopped
1 cup peas
2 cups medium seashell noodles
½ cup chopped parsley

Place hen, celery, onion, bay leaf, nutmeg and salt and pepper in soup pot, and cover with cold water. Bring to a boil, reduce heat, and simmer for 3 hours. Remove chicken, cool slightly, and remove meat from bones.

Add meat, green onions, carrots, peas and noodles, and boil for 15 minutes, or until carrots and noodles are tender. Add parsley and serve.

Serves 8 to 10.

— *Anneliese Range*
Grande Prairie, Alberta

PESTO SOUP

PESTO IS A THICK PASTE MADE ESSENTIALLY FROM GROUND BASIL, WHICH can be served over pasta or added to other dishes, such as this soup, as a seasoning.

1 Tbsp. oil
4 leeks, thinly sliced
1 large onion, sliced
4 tomatoes, skinned & chopped
1 large clove garlic, crushed
¾ cup chopped mixed herbs (parsley, chervil, tarragon)
Salt & pepper
½ lb. green beans, sliced
4 small zucchini, sliced
½ cup cauliflower florets
7 cups boiling chicken stock
¼ lb. vermicelli
1 cup cooked navy beans
½ cup pesto, page 97
1 cup Parmesan cheese

Heat oil in heavy, deep pot. Add leeks, onion, tomatoes, garlic, herbs and salt and pepper. Cook gently for 15 minutes, then stir in beans, zucchini and cauliflower. Cover with boiling stock and cook for 5 minutes. Add vermicelli and beans.

When vermicelli is tender, remove soup from heat. Stir in pesto and serve garnished with Parmesan cheese.

Serves 6.

— Katherine Dunster
Golden, British Columbia

ITALIAN LENTIL SOUP

3 onions, chopped
3 cloves garlic, minced
4 Tbsp. butter
1 cup green lentils
64-oz. can tomato juice
1 tsp. basil
½ tsp. oregano
Salt & pepper
½ cup broken raw spaghetti

Sauté onions and garlic in butter until translucent. Add lentils, tomato juice, basil, oregano and salt and pepper. Bring to a boil, cover, then simmer gently until lentils are tender — 2 to 3 hours. Add pasta and simmer for 15 more minutes.

Serves 4 to 6.

— Tobi Gillespie
Manotick, Ontario

MINESTRONE

Minestrone is a general term referring to a thick vegetable soup. This one, from the Tuscan region, incorporates pasta instead of potatoes or rice.

1½ cups navy beans
3 Tbsp. olive oil
1 large onion, chopped
3 cloves garlic, crushed
4 Tbsp. chopped parsley
1 Tbsp. chopped thyme
1 Tbsp. chopped rosemary
1 cup sliced celery
½ cup sliced carrots
1 bay leaf
2 cups canned tomatoes
½ cup Spicy Tomato Sauce, page 96
1½ cups chopped zucchini
1 cup shredded cabbage
2 cups shredded Swiss chard
Salt & pepper
1 cup small-shell pasta
1 cup Parmesan cheese

Soak beans overnight in 4 cups water. Rinse beans, then cook in 5 cups water for 1 hour, or until cooked but still firm. Drain beans, reserving liquid. Set both aside.

Meanwhile, heat olive oil in heavy pot, and sauté onions and garlic until golden. Add parsley, thyme and rosemary, and cook for 1 more minute. Add celery, carrots and bay leaf and cook, stirring, for 3 minutes. Add tomatoes and Spicy Tomato Sauce, reduce heat, and simmer for 30 minutes.

Mash 1 cup of the beans to a smooth pulp and add, along with cooking liquid, to tomato mixture. Simmer for 15 minutes. Add zucchini, cabbage, Swiss chard and remaining beans, and simmer for 20 minutes, or until vegetables and beans are tender.

Add water if needed to make approximately 6 cups of liquid. Add salt and pepper to taste, and pasta. Cook for 10 minutes or until pasta is cooked. Serve garnished with Parmesan cheese.

Serves 6.

MEATBALL NOODLE SOUP

10 cups water
1 onion
1 bay leaf
10 peppercorns
1 sprig parsley
Salt
1 lb. ground beef
1 egg
9 Tbsp. flour
4 potatoes, diced
2 eggs
⅛ tsp. salt
Milk
½ cup butter
Light cream

Bring water, onion, bay leaf, peppercorns, parsley and salt to a boil, reduce heat and simmer.

Meanwhile, combine beef, egg and 1 Tbsp. flour, and form into small meatballs. Brown and drain off fat. Remove spices from stock.

Add meatballs and potatoes, reduce heat, and cook until potatoes are done.

While this is cooking, combine eggs, salt, remaining 8 Tbsp. flour and enough milk to make a soft dough. Knead gently on floured board. Roll out to ¼-inch thickness, cut into strips, then use scissors to cut strips into short noodles.

Add to soup and cook for 10 to 15 minutes. Add butter and cream to taste.

Serves 6.

— Judy Trimble
McLaughlin, Alberta

CHICKEN SOUP WITH VERMICELLI

1 Tbsp. oil
½-inch slice ginger root, chopped
3 lbs. chicken, cut up
4 sprigs parsley
¼ tsp. salt
¼ tsp. pepper
4 oz. vermicelli
2 Tbsp. sherry
2 Tbsp. tamari sauce
½ lb. snow peas, sliced in half crosswise
1 green onion, thinly sliced

Heat oil, and sauté ginger until golden brown. Add chicken pieces, parsley, salt and pepper, and cover with cold water. Cover and bring to a boil. Reduce heat, and simmer for 1 to 2 hours, or until chicken is tender and broth rich. Remove chicken, and strain stock, skimming off excess fat. When chicken has cooled, remove meat from bones, and finely chop.

Measure stock and add water to make 6 cups. Stir in vermicelli, sherry and tamari sauce, bring to a boil, and cook until noodles are tender. Stir in chicken and snow peas, and cook, uncovered, for another 1 to 2 minutes. Sprinkle with green onion, and serve.

Serves 4 to 6.

SPÄTZLE

THESE DROP NOODLES MAKE A DELICIOUS ADDITION TO SOUPS AND STEWS. They can be cooked as indicated below and served, buttered, with a stew, or can be cooked directly in a soup.

2⅓ cups flour
1 tsp. salt
1 egg, slightly beaten
1 cup water

Sift together flour and salt. Combine egg and water, and stir into flour until dough is thick and smooth.

Bring 2 quarts water to a boil. Using a spoon dipped in cold water, spoon ½-tsp. bits of dough into water, being careful not to crowd. After noodles rise to the surface, boil for 5 to 8 minutes or until soft.

— Nora Scott
Millgrove, Ontario

SALADS

The summer's gift, a cherished prize in winter

DILLED SHRIMP & CAPPELLINI SALAD

½ cup dry white wine
⅓ cup white wine vinegar
1½ cups olive oil
3 Tbsp. finely chopped dill weed
2 tsp. salt
Pepper
1½ lbs. shrimp, shelled, cooked & sliced lengthwise in half
1½ lbs. cappellini, cooked, drained & rinsed

Combine wine, vinegar, oil, dill, salt and pepper, and mix well. Add shrimp, and let marinate for a least 30 minutes. Pour over cappellini, toss to coat well, and serve.

Serves 6.

PASTA SALAD NIÇOISE

⅓ cup oil
3 Tbsp. lemon juice
3 Tbsp. vinegar
½ tsp. salt
½ tsp. dry mustard
½ tsp. paprika
½ tsp. basil
8 oz. linguine
1 cup sliced green beans, cooked, drained & chilled
1 cup halved cherry tomatoes
¼ cup sliced, pitted ripe olives
12½-oz. can tuna, chilled & drained
3 hard-cooked eggs, sliced

To make dressing, combine oil, lemon juice, vinegar, salt, mustard, paprika and basil in a screw-top jar. Cover, and shake well to mix.

Cook linguine, drain, and rinse under cold water. Pour dressing over linguine, and toss gently to coat. Cover, and chill for several hours.

Combine chilled linguine, green beans, cherry tomatoes and olives in salad bowl, tossing to mix. Break tuna into bite-sized chunks, and mound on top of salad. Garnish with sliced eggs.

Serves 6.

— Christine Taylor
Norbertville, Quebec

TOMATO MOZZARELLA PASTA SALAD

1 clove garlic, peeled
½ lb. tripolini, cooked, drained & cooled
4 large tomatoes, quartered
½ lb. mozzarella cheese, cut into ¼-inch cubes
1 green pepper, sliced into rings
12 black olives, pitted & halved
12 large basil leaves, chopped
1 purple onion, sliced into rings
½ cup olive oil
½ tsp. oregano
Salt & pepper
Basil leaves to garnish

Rub wooden salad bowl with garlic. Discard garlic. Add tripolini, tomatoes, cheese, green pepper, olives, basil, onion, oil, oregano and salt and pepper.

Toss well. Garnish with whole basil leaves.

Serves 4.

SALMON BROCCOLI SALAD

4 cups raw bow noodles
1 bunch broccoli
⅓ cup oil
3 Tbsp. lemon juice
¼ tsp. dry mustard
1 Tbsp. fresh dill weed
1 cup cooked, flaked salmon
Salt & pepper

Cook noodles until just tender. Break broccoli into bite-sized pieces, and cook until tender-crisp. Drain and rinse with cold water.

Meanwhile, prepare dressing. Whisk together oil, lemon juice, dry mustard and dill.

Mix dressing with noodles, and stir to coat. Stir in broccoli and salmon. Add salt and pepper to taste. Cover bowl, and refrigerate until well chilled — about 3 hours.

Serves 8.

— Lynn Hill
Barry's Bay, Ontario

KIELBASA & ROTINI SALAD WITH DIJON MAYONNAISE

2 cups cooked rotini
1 cup chopped Kielbasa sausage
½ cup chopped green pepper
½ cup chopped sweet red pepper
½ cup chopped celery
3 green onions, chopped
2 eggs
2 Tbsp. Dijon mustard
¼ cup olive oil
1-1¼ cups vegetable oil
Lemon juice
Salt & pepper

Combine rotini, sausage, peppers, celery and green onions.

Place eggs and mustard in food processor and blend. With processor running slowly, pour in oils until thick and white. Add lemon juice and salt and pepper to taste.

Toss with salad and chill well.

Serves 4.

CURRIED PASTA SALAD

4 carrots, sliced
4 oz. farfalle
1 green pepper, julienned
12 snow peas, halved
¼ cup vinegar
2 Tbsp. olive oil
1 tsp. curry
⅛ tsp. salt
Pepper
½ cup peanuts

Cook carrots in enough boiling water to just cover for 5 to 10 minutes or until tender-crisp. Drain and cool.

Meanwhile, cook farfalle. Drain, and rinse in cold water. Toss together with carrots, green pepper and snow peas.

Combine vinegar, oil, curry, salt and pepper, and shake well. Pour over salad and toss. Cover and chill for several hours. Toss with peanuts before serving.

Serves 4.

DILLY PASTA SALAD

4 oz. farfalle, cooked, drained & rinsed in cold water
½ cup grated Monterey Jack cheese
⅓ cup sliced celery
½ green pepper, julienned
2 Tbsp. chopped green olives
½ cup mayonnaise
1 Tbsp. chopped fresh dill weed
⅛ tsp. salt

Combine farfalle, cheese, celery, green pepper and olives. Mix together mayonnaise, dill and salt, and pour over salad. Toss to coat. Chill for several hours or overnight.

Serves 6.

LYNN'S PASTA SALAD

1 cup mayonnaise
½ cup parsley
¼ cup Parmesan cheese
2 Tbsp. lemon juice
1 clove garlic, minced
1 tsp. basil
2 cups cooked macaroni
1 cup cooked kidney beans
1 cup diced, cooked carrots
1 cup peas

Combine mayonnaise, parsley, cheese, lemon juice, garlic and basil for dressing.

Place macaroni, beans, carrots and peas in bowl. Add dressing and toss to mix well. Chill for several hours before serving.

Serves 4.

— Dianne Baker
Tatamagouche, Nova Scotia

SHRIMP & PASTA SALAD

5 cups small pasta shells, cooked
2 cups cooked shrimp
¾ cup finely diced Gouda cheese
¾ cup finely diced colby cheese
½ cup diced dill pickles
1 cup cooked peas
½ cup finely chopped green onions
¾ cup mayonnaise
½ cup yogurt
¼ cup French dressing
1 tsp. dill weed
1 tsp. lemon juice
Pepper

Combine pasta, shrimp, cheeses, dill pickles, peas and green onions. Combine mayonnaise, yogurt, dressing, dill weed, lemon juice and pepper, and mix well.

Fold carefully into shrimp mixture. Chill well.

Serves 8.

— Shelley Townsend
Lethbridge, Alberta

MACARONI SALAD

2 cups uncooked macaroni
1 cup sliced celery
½ cup chopped green onions
¼ cup sliced radishes
1 cup cubed Cheddar cheese
¾ cup mayonnaise
1 Tbsp. vinegar
1 tsp. mustard
1 tsp. salt
Pepper

Cook the macaroni. Drain and rinse with cold water until cool. Toss together the cooked macaroni, vegetables and cheese.

Mix together the mayonnaise, vinegar, mustard, salt and pepper. Toss dressing together with salad. Refrigerate.

Serves 6 to 8.

— Bertha Geddert
Ft. McMurray, Alberta

NOODLE SALAD

AN EXCELLENT AND EASY WAY TO USE UP LEFTOVER PASTA, THIS DISH CAN
even utilize pasta with sauce on it — just rinse thoroughly in cold water
before mixing with dressing.

½ cup yogurt
½ cup mayonnaise
1 Tbsp. Dijon mustard
1 Tbsp. dill weed
3-4 cups cooked pasta

Combine yogurt, mayonnaise, mustard and dill. Mix with rinsed pasta,
and chill well.

Serves 4.

CASSEROLES

A hearty dish and piping hot can melt the winter's frost

WHITE LASAGNE

15-18 lasagne noodles
1 lb. spinach or mustard greens, chopped & briefly cooked
4 eggs, lightly beaten
1 lb. ricotta cheese
Salt & pepper
Nutmeg
5 Tbsp. butter
¼ cup chopped onion
1 large clove garlic, crushed
4 Tbsp. flour
2 cups hot milk
¾ cup Parmesan cheese
12 oz. mozzarella cheese, grated

Cook lasagne, uncovered, in boiling, salted water for 4 to 5 minutes. Drain.

Combine spinach or mustard greens, eggs and ricotta cheese, and mix well. Season with salt and pepper and nutmeg.

Melt 1 Tbsp. butter, and cook onion and garlic until limp. Stir into spinach mixture.

Melt remaining butter, and stir in flour to make a roux. Add hot milk all at once and beat. Stir in ½ cup Parmesan cheese and heat, stirring, until thickened. Remove from heat and set aside.

Place a third of the noodles, overlapping each other, in the bottom of a greased 9″ x 13″ casserole dish. Spread half the spinach mixture over this, then a third of the mozzarella cheese. Season with pepper. Repeat. Place a third layer of noodles over all, then pour cheese sauce over this, and top with remaining mozzarella and Parmesan cheese. Season with pepper and a little nutmeg.

Bake at 350 degrees F for 35 minutes. Let stand for 30 minutes before serving.

Serves 6.

AREZZO LASAGNE

THIS DISH IS NAMED FOR THE CITY IN CENTRAL ITALY WHERE IT originated.

1 recipe Basic Pasta Dough, page 23
1 medium duck
2 cups dry red wine
8 cups chicken stock
2 carrots, finely chopped
2 stalks celery, finely chopped
1 onion, quartered
2 leeks, finely chopped
½ cup chopped parsley
1 Tbsp. chopped tarragon
Handful sorrel
4 cups grated mild cheese (e.g. mozzarella)
Butter
2 cups béchamel sauce
Nutmeg

Prepare Basic Pasta Dough, cover with a damp cloth, and set aside.

Place duck in large, heavy pot with wine, stock, carrots, celery, onion, leeks, parsley, tarragon and sorrel. Stew until meat falls off bones, then remove from pot. Strain stock and set aside.

Remove meat from bones and chop it finely. Add enough stock to make a thick meat sauce.

Roll out dough and cut into lasagne noodles. Assemble dish by layering pasta, meat sauce, cheese, dots of butter and then ending with pasta. Top with béchamel sauce, a grating of nutmeg and dots of butter.

Bake at 350 degrees F for 30 minutes.

Serves 6.

AUTHENTIC ITALIAN LASAGNE

"ONE AFTERNOON YEARS AGO, I WATCHED AS AN ITALIAN NEIGHBOUR — who spoke no English — prepared this recipe. My daughter, Dianne, had raved about the lasagne that "Tony's mother" made, so armed with pencil and paper and my broken Italian, I set about getting this recipe for 'authentic' Italian lasagne down on paper. We have been enjoying it ever since."

⅓ cup olive oil
1 large onion, chopped
1 lb. ground beef
28-oz. can plum tomatoes
5½-oz. can tomato paste
1 tsp. oregano
¼ tsp. hot red pepper seeds
Salt & pepper
1 lb. lasagne
1 Tbsp. salt
1 lb. mozzarella cheese
⅓ lb. Parmesan cheese
¼ lb. old Cheddar cheese
2 hard-boiled eggs

Heat oil in large skillet, add onion, and sauté. Add meat, and brown slightly. Add tomatoes, tomato paste, oregano, hot pepper seeds and salt and pepper. Simmer, uncovered, for 30 minutes or until thick.

Cook lasagne for 15 minutes in boiling water. Drain and return to pot with a teaspoon of oil so noodles will not stick together.

Grate cheeses, setting aside ¼ cup Parmesan. Mix cheeses together carefully with eggs. Place a little sauce in the bottom of a greased 9" x 13" baking dish. Layer ingredients as follows: lasagne, cheese mixture and sauce. Repeat. End with a layer of lasagne topped with sauce and the remaining Parmesan.

Cover with foil. Bake at 325 degrees F for 45 minutes. Uncover and brown at 550 degrees for 10 to 15 minutes. Let stand for 10 minutes before cutting and serving.

Serves 6.

— *Anna Dickinson*
Downsview, Ontario

NEAPOLITAN LASAGNE

1 lb. ground beef
2 hot Italian sausages, out of casings
1 large onion, finely chopped
1 stalk celery, finely chopped
2 cloves garlic, minced
4 cups puréed canned tomatoes
6-oz. can tomato paste
4 oz. dry red wine
1 tsp. marjoram
1 tsp. basil
Parsley
½ tsp. cinnamon
Salt & pepper
2 eggs
2 cups cottage cheese
¾ cup Parmesan cheese
16 lasagne noodles, cooked
1 lb. spinach, cooked, drained & chopped
1 zucchini, thinly sliced
½ lb. mozzarella cheese, thinly sliced

In heavy pot, cook beef, sausage meat, onion, celery and garlic until lightly browned. Stir in puréed tomatoes and paste, then wine, marjoram, basil, parsley, cinnamon and salt and pepper. Simmer for 30 minutes. Meanwhile, combine eggs, cottage cheese and ½ cup Parmesan cheese.

Place a little sauce on the bottom of greased 9″ x 13″ pan. Alternate layers as follows: noodles, cheese mixture, spinach and zucchini slices, mozzarella, meat sauce. Repeat. Sprinkle with remaining ¼ cup Parmesan cheese. Bake at 375 degrees F for 30 minutes.

Serves 10 to 12.

— *Valerie Marien*
Orangeville, Ontario

VEGETABLE LASAGNE

ZUCCHINI AND OLIVES PROVIDE ANOTHER INTERESTING VARIATION TO THE standard lasagne flavour. This recipe can be frozen with no detraction from the original flavour.

1 large clove garlic, minced
2 Tbsp. oil
1 large onion, chopped
1 green pepper, chopped
2 stalks celery, chopped
½ tsp. oregano
½ tsp. basil
½ tsp. thyme
1 medium zucchini, coarsely grated
1½ cups sliced mushrooms
1½ cups Spicy Tomato Sauce, page 96
¼ cup Parmesan cheese
8 oz. lasagne, cooked
2 cups cottage cheese, mixed with 1 egg
10 oz. spinach, torn into 1-inch pieces
2 cups grated mozzarella cheese
½ cup chopped black olives

Sauté garlic in oil for 1 minute. Add onion, green pepper, celery and herbs, and cook for 5 minutes. Add zucchini and cook for another 5 minutes. Add mushrooms and Spicy Tomato Sauce. Simmer for 20 minutes, remove from heat, add Parmesan cheese, and mix well.

Spread a small amount of the sauce in the bottom of a greased 2-quart casserole dish. Layer in half of each of the ingredients: noodles, sauce, cottage cheese, spinach, mozzarella cheese and olives. Repeat.

Cover and bake for 1 hour at 350 degrees F. Allow to sit for 10 minutes before serving.

Serves 6 to 8.

— Shan Simpson
Leslieville, Alberta

TOFU LASAGNE

THE SUBSTITUTION OF TOFU FOR GROUND BEEF IN THIS RECIPE ALLOWS vegetarians to enjoy a delicious, protein-rich lasagne. Wheat germ adds a slightly nutty flavour.

8 oz. lasagne
¼ cup butter
½ lb. mushrooms, thinly sliced
3 cloves garlic, minced
½ tsp. salt
⅛ tsp. pepper
3 cups Spicy Tomato Sauce, page 96
½ cup wheat germ
1 cup mashed tofu
¼ cup Parmesan cheese
½ lb. mozzarella cheese, grated
¼ cup chopped parsley

Cook and drain lasagne. Set aside.

Melt butter in large skillet. Add mushrooms, garlic, salt and pepper. Cook until mushrooms are tender. Stir in Spicy Tomato Sauce and wheat germ. Heat through.

Combine tofu and Parmesan cheese in a bowl. Combine mozzarella and parsley in another bowl.

In a 9″ x 12″ pan, layer half of each of the ingredients: noodles, tofu mixture, sauce and mozzarella mixture. Repeat.

Bake at 350 degrees F for 45 minutes or until hot and bubbly. Let stand for 15 minutes before cutting.

Serves 8 to 10.

— *Pat Bredin*
Winnipeg, Manitoba

SALMON LASAGNE

AN UNUSUAL ADAPTATION OF TRADITIONAL LASAGNE, THIS RECIPE CAN BE quickly assembled and will feed a crowd.

¼ cup butter
½ cup chopped onion
½ cup chopped green pepper
2½ cups canned tomatoes
1 tsp. basil
½ tsp. salt
2 lbs. cooked, boned & flaked salmon
8 oz. lasagne, cooked
½ lb. mozzarella cheese, sliced
½ cup Parmesan cheese

Melt butter, and sauté onion and green pepper until tender but not browned. Add tomatoes, basil, salt and salmon. Mix gently.

Arrange layers of noodles, salmon and cheeses, making 3 layers, with the cheese on top, in a greased 12" x 14" pan.

Bake at 375 degrees F for 25 to 30 minutes, or until cheese is bubbly.

Serves 10 to 12.

— Irene Louden
Port Coquitlam, British Columbia

PUMPKIN LASAGNE

THIS RECIPE PROVIDES AN UNUSUAL BUT TASTY WAY OF COPING WITH
an overabundance of pumpkin.

½ lb. spinach noodles
4 Tbsp. butter
2 Tbsp. chopped onion
3 Tbsp. flour
2 cups milk
⅛ tsp. nutmeg
Salt
Cayenne
2 cups cooked, mashed pumpkin
1 cup dry cottage cheese
¼ cup yogurt
3 eggs
¾ cup Parmesan cheese
Nutmeg
Salt & pepper
Chopped parsley

Cook noodles, drain, rinse in cold water, and set aside.

Melt butter, and sauté onion until limp. Stir in flour, cook for 2 minutes on
low heat, then gradually whisk in milk. Continue cooking and stirring
until sauce is smooth and thick. Add nutmeg, salt and cayenne.

Combine pumpkin, cottage cheese, yogurt, eggs, ½ cup Parmesan cheese,
nutmeg and salt and pepper. Layer noodles, filling and sauce in greased
9" x 13" pan, finishing with sauce. Sprinkle with remaining Parmesan
cheese, and bake at 350 degrees F for 30 minutes, or until golden and
bubbly. Garnish with parsley and serve.

Serves 6.

— Heather Quiney
Victoria, British Columbia

PASTA ESPAÑOLE

Sauce
2 Tbsp. oil
1 onion, chopped
4 cups canned tomatoes
6½-oz. can tomato paste
1 clove garlic, crushed
1 bay leaf
1 Tbsp. chopped basil
1 tsp. marjoram
1 tsp. salt
¼ tsp. hot chilies
Pepper

Filling
2 Tbsp. oil
1 onion, chopped
1 lb. ground beef
1 clove garlic, crushed
1 tsp. oregano
1 tsp. salt
¼ tsp. dill weed
¼ tsp. pepper
½ tsp. parsley
½ cup sliced mushrooms

6 lasagne noodles
1 cup cottage cheese
½ cup grated mozzarella cheese

To make sauce, heat oil and sauté onion. Stir in remaining sauce ingredients, bring to a boil, then simmer for 20 minutes. Remove bay leaf.

Meanwhile, prepare filling. Heat oil, and sauté onion until limp. Add ground beef and cook until browned. Drain off fat. Add garlic, oregano, salt, dill weed, pepper, parsley and mushrooms. Simmer for 15 minutes.

Cook lasagne, drain, and cut in half.

Place a generous spoonful of filling along with a spoonful of cottage cheese on each lasagne half. Fold ends over mixture. Place in greased shallow baking dish, seam side down. Top with sauce and mozzarella cheese.

Bake at 350 degrees F for 30 minutes.

Serves 4.

— Helen Shepherd
Lansdowne, Ontario

THREE CHEESE CANNELLONI

Cannelloni can be made with homemade crepes, as this recipe indicates, or with commercial pasta.

6 eggs
1½ cups flour
¼ tsp. salt
2 lbs. ricotta cheese
½ lb. mozzarella cheese
⅓ cup Parmesan cheese
2 eggs
1 tsp. salt
¼ tsp. pepper
1 Tbsp. chopped parsley
¼ cup Parmesan cheese
2-3 cups Spicy Tomato Sauce, page 96

Combine eggs, flour, salt and 1½ cups water in blender. After blending, let stand 30 minutes or longer.

Grease and heat an 8-inch skillet. Pour in 3 Tbsp. of batter, rotating skillet quickly to spread batter evenly. Cook over medium heat until top is dry. Cool on wire rack, then stack with wax paper between crêpes.

For filling, combine all remaining ingredients except ¼ cup of Parmesan cheese and Spicy Tomato Sauce. Beat with a wooden spoon to blend well. Spread about ¼ cup filling down the centre of each crêpe, and roll up. Place completed rolls, seam side down, in a shallow casserole dish, making 2 layers if necessary. Top with Spicy Tomato Sauce and remaining Parmesan cheese.

Bake at 350 degrees F for 30 minutes.

Serves 8.

— Hazel R. Baker
Coombs, British Columbia

CHICKEN CANNELLONI

3 chicken breasts
12 cannelloni noodles
6 Tbsp. butter
5 Tbsp. flour
4 cups milk
Salt & pepper
1½ cups sliced mushrooms
2 cloves garlic, chopped
½ tsp. salt
1 tsp. paprika
1 cup liverwurst
½ cup Parmesan cheese

Cook chicken breasts in water until tender but still moist. Remove breasts from stock to cool, then take meat off bones and mash it. (A food processor makes this very simple, but it can be done by hand using a wooden pestle.)

Melt 4 Tbsp. butter, stir in flour and then milk to make a white sauce. Add salt and pepper to taste.

Melt remaining 2 Tbsp. butter in heavy skillet, and sauté mushrooms and garlic. Add salt, paprika, liverwurst and chicken. Stir in just enough white sauce to make mixture stick together, and add ¼ cup Parmesan cheese.

Coat bottom of 9″ x 13″ pan with a little white sauce. Place chicken mixture in a pastry tube, and stuff cannelloni. Place in pan, cover with remaining white sauce, and top with remaining cheese.

Bake at 350 degrees F for 20 to 30 minutes or until lightly browned.

Serves 4.

— Bonny Jordan
Merrickville, Ontario

SPINACH BEEF MANICOTTI

2 cups chopped onion
¼ cup butter
¾ lb. fresh spinach
4 cloves garlic, minced
2 tsp. oregano
Salt & pepper
1 lb. ground beef
2 Tbsp. oil
32-oz. can tomatoes
6-oz. can tomato paste
1 Tbsp. basil
12 manicotti shells, cooked, drained & cooled
½ cup Parmesan cheese

Sauté 1½ cups of the onion in butter for 5 minutes. Tear spinach into 1-inch pieces, and add to onion along with 2 cloves garlic, oregano and salt and pepper. Stir-fry 2 to 3 minutes, then add ground beef. Cook until beef is thoroughly browned. Set aside.

Sauté remaining onion in oil until soft. Stir in tomatoes, tomato paste, remaining garlic, basil and salt and pepper. Bring to a boil, reduce heat, cover, and simmer for 20 minutes.

Stuff shells with meat filling, and place in a shallow baking dish. Cover with tomato sauce, and sprinkle with Parmesan cheese.

Bake at 350 degrees F for 30 minutes.

Serves 6.

— Bryanna Clark
Union Bay, British Columbia

MEAT-STUFFED MANICOTTI
WITH TOMATO SAUCE

Filling
½ cup chopped onions
1 clove garlic, minced
3 Tbsp. oil
¾ lb. ground beef
6-8 oz. cooked, chopped spinach
¼ cup Parmesan cheese
1 egg, beaten
½ tsp. oregano
½ tsp. salt
Pepper

8 manicotti shells, cooked

Sauce
1 clove garlic, minced
1 Tbsp. oil
28-oz. can tomatoes
1½ tsp. basil
½ tsp. salt
Pepper
Parmesan cheese

Brown onions and garlic in oil. Add ground beef and brown. Add spinach, and cook for 5 minutes. Remove excess liquid, then add remaining ingredients. Stuff manicotti shells with this mixture, and place in greased baking dish.

To make sauce, sauté garlic in oil. Coarsely chop tomatoes, and add along with juice and seasonings. Bring to a boil, reduce heat, and simmer for 20 to 30 minutes, until sauce has reached desired consistency. Pour over manicotti, and sprinkle with Parmesan cheese.

Bake at 350 degrees F for 25 minutes.

Serves 4.

— Donna Parker
Pictou, Nova Scotia

PASTA PIE

Pastry for double-crust pie
4 Tbsp. butter
4 Tbsp. flour
4 cups light cream
Salt & pepper
2 cups grated Swiss cheese
2 cups rotini, cooked

Prepare pastry, roll out bottom crust, and line pie plate.

Melt butter, and stir in flour until smooth. Slowly add cream, stirring constantly, and cook until thickened. Add salt and pepper and cheese. Cook, stirring, until cheese has melted and sauce is thick and smooth.

Mix together rotini and cheese sauce. Pour into pie crust, top with remaining pastry, slash top to allow steam to escape, and bake at 350 degrees F for 20 to 30 minutes, or until golden brown.

Serves 4 to 6.

SPINACH NOODLE CUSTARD

1 lb. rotini
4 Tbsp. butter
3-4 green onions, minced
2 bunches spinach, cooked, drained & chopped
2 cups cheese sauce
1 pint sour cream
2 eggs
Salt & pepper
Parmesan cheese

Cook rotini and drain well. Melt butter, add onions and cook, stirring, until limp. Remove from heat, and add spinach, cheese sauce, sour cream, eggs and salt and pepper.

Toss noodles in this, then place in greased casserole dish, and sprinkle with Parmesan cheese. Bake at 350 degrees F for 35 minutes.

Serves 6.

— Valerie Gillis
Renfrew, Ontario

ITALIAN CHICKEN & PASTA

1 Tbsp. butter
1 Tbsp. oil
6 pieces chicken
3 onions
1 cup chicken stock
1 cup dry white wine
2 cloves garlic
½ tsp. oregano
Pepper
2-oz. can anchovy fillets or 2 Tbsp. anchovy paste
2 Tbsp. cornstarch dissolved in 2 Tbsp. cold water
¼ cup pimento cut into narrow strips
½ cup pitted black olives
¾ lb. rotini, cooked, drained, buttered & tossed with Parmesan cheese

Heat butter and oil in large skillet, and sauté chicken pieces until golden. Remove from skillet, and place in large casserole dish with tight-fitting lid.

Cut onions into quarters, and sauté until lightly browned. Place on top of chicken. Drain fat from skillet, add stock, wine, garlic, oregano and pepper, and bring to a boil.

Drain anchovies, chop finely, then mash into a paste, and stir into sauce. Thicken with cornstarch dissolved in water. Pour over chicken, and bake, covered, for 30 minutes. Sprinkle pimento and olives over chicken, and bake for another 15 minutes.

Serve with rotini.

Serves 6.

— Joann Alho
Brantford, Ontario

SPAGHETTI WITH SPINACH, MUSHROOMS & CREAM

SERVED WITH A SALAD AND A PRUNE SOUFFLE, THIS MAKES A DELICIOUS light meal.

4 cups spinach, stemmed, chopped & cooked until wilted
½ lb. mushrooms, trimmed & sliced
1 cup whipping cream
3 Tbsp. lemon juice
4 Tbsp. butter
1 clove garlic, crushed
2 Tbsp. Marsala
Salt & pepper
½ lb. spaghetti, cooked
⅓ cup Parmesan cheese

Combine spinach, mushrooms, whipping cream, lemon juice, butter, garlic, Marsala and salt and pepper. Mix well and toss with spaghetti. Place in greased baking dish, top with Parmesan cheese, and bake at 350 degrees F for 20 to 30 minutes, or until hot.

Serves 6.

— *Nicky Webb*
Bridesville, British Columbia

PENNE WITH CRAB & SHRIMP SAUCE

12 oz. penne
8 oz. shrimp
8 oz. crab
¼ cup butter
1 tsp. curry
¼ cup flour
¼ tsp. salt
¼ tsp. pepper
2 cups milk
½ cup grated mozzarella cheese
Parmesan cheese

Cook and drain penne. Sauté shrimp and crab in butter and curry for 3 to 4 minutes. Blend in flour, salt and pepper. Gradually stir in milk and mozzarella cheese, and cook until thick.

Pour sauce over penne, stir, and place in greased casserole dish. Sprinkle with Parmesan cheese. Bake at 350 degrees F until bubbly hot, then broil to brown cheese.

Serves 6.

— *Carrol Chura*
Victoria, British Columbia

SPAGHETTI PEANUT CASSEROLE

2 cups spaghetti, cooked
½ cup sliced black olives
1 cup grated Cheddar cheese
1 cup chopped peanuts
3 Tbsp. butter
3 Tbsp. flour
1 tsp. salt
1 tsp. dry mustard
¼ tsp. pepper
2 cups buttermilk
½ cup chopped onion
Tabasco sauce
⅓ cup bread crumbs

In greased 2-quart casserole, layer spaghetti, olives, cheese and peanuts, using half of each. Repeat layers.

Melt butter. Add flour, salt, mustard and pepper, and cook, stirring, for 2 minutes. Gradually, whisk in buttermilk, and cook until thickened. Add onion and Tabasco sauce. Pour over casserole.

Top with bread crumbs, and bake at 350 degrees F for 25 minutes.

Serves 4.

— Heather Quiney
Victoria, British Columbia

SPAGHETTI SERENE

8 oz. spaghetti
1 Tbsp. oil
1½ lbs. ground beef
1 tsp. salt
¼ tsp. pepper
2 cups Spicy Tomato Sauce, page 96
¼ cup chopped green onion
8 oz. cream cheese
2 cups cottage cheese
½ cup sour cream

Cook spaghetti, drain, and place half in greased 2-quart casserole dish.

To make meat sauce, heat oil and brown beef. Drain off fat and discard. Add salt, pepper, Spicy Tomato Sauce and onions, and set aside.

Combine cream cheese, cottage cheese and sour cream in bowl, mixing well. Spoon over spaghetti in casserole, cover with remaining spaghetti, and top with meat mixture.

Bake at 350 degrees F for 45 minutes.

Serves 6 to 8.

— Judy Trimble
McLaughlin, Alberta

EGGPLANT & MOZZARELLA CASSEROLE

3 medium eggplants
Coarse salt
1 lb. mezze zite
8 Tbsp. butter
4 cups Spicy Tomato Sauce, page 96
½ lb. mozzarella cheese, thinly sliced
Parmesan cheese

Wash eggplants. Cut into ½-inch slices, sprinkle with salt, weight with a heavy plate, and leave to drain for a few hours.

Cook the zite until just tender, drain, and mix with 4 Tbsp. butter and Spicy Tomato Sauce.

Grease a casserole dish, and fill with layers of zite, eggplant and mozzarella cheese, ending with cheese. Dot with remaining butter, and sprinkle with Parmesan cheese.

Bake at 350 degrees F for 45 minutes.

Serves 6.

— Nicky Webb
Bridesville, British Columbia

CHEESY FISH WITH SPINACH NOODLES

1 cup water
½ tsp. salt
2 lbs. fish fillets
2 onions, thinly sliced
4 stalks celery, chopped
1 cup sliced mushrooms
6 Tbsp. butter
3 Tbsp. flour
2½ cups light cream
Salt & pepper
1 cup grated sharp Cheddar cheese
1 lb. spinach fettuccine
Butter

Bring salted water to a boil, add fish, and simmer for 10 minutes, or until fish is cooked. In heavy skillet, sauté onions, celery and mushrooms in 3 Tbsp. butter until limp. Remove and set aside. Add remaining butter to pan. When melted, stir in flour and cook for 2 minutes. Add cream slowly and cook until thick. Season to taste. Arrange fish in greased casserole dish, top with vegetables, and pour sauce over it all. Sprinkle with grated cheese.

Bake at 375 degrees F for 15 minutes or until hot and bubbly.

Meanwhile, cook noodles until just tender, drain, rinse, and toss with butter.

Serve noodles topped with fish.

Serves 6 to 8.

— Leslie Hawkins
Thunder Bay, Ontario

SPAGHETTI PIE

6 oz. spaghetti
2 Tbsp. butter
¾ cup grated mozzarella cheese
2 eggs, beaten
3 Tbsp. oil
½ cup chopped onion
¼ cup chopped green pepper
1 lb. ground beef
1 cup chopped tomatoes
6-oz. can tomato paste
1 tsp. oregano
½ tsp. basil
1 clove garlic, minced
1 cup dry cottage cheese

Cook spaghetti and drain. Stir butter into hot noodles, then stir in ¼ cup mozzarella cheese and eggs. Press mixture into greased 10-inch pie plate to form a crust.

Heat oil, and sauté onion and green pepper until just tender. Add meat and brown. Stir in tomatoes, tomato paste, oregano, basil and garlic, and remove from heat.

Spread cottage cheese over crust. Fill pie with tomato mixture, cover with foil, and chill for several hours. Bake, covered, at 350 degrees F for 1 hour. Uncover, sprinkle with remaining mozzarella cheese, and bake for 5 more minutes.

Serves 4.

— Dianne Baker
Tatamagouche, Nova Scotia

BAKED STUFFED PASTA SHELLS

18 jumbo pasta shells
4 cups washed, trimmed, packed spinach
Oil
2 Tbsp. diced celery
3 Tbsp. diced onion
2 Tbsp. finely chopped fresh mushrooms
1 cup cottage cheese
1 egg
Pepper
½ tsp. marjoram
½ tsp. dill weed
3 Tbsp. flour
¼ tsp. dry mustard
Nutmeg
2½ cups milk
½ cup grated sharp Cheddar cheese

Cook pasta. Drain, rinse with cold water, and drain again. Cook spinach over high heat until wilted – about 2 minutes. Drain, chop, and place in medium-sized bowl.

Heat 2-3 Tbsp. oil in heavy skillet over medium heat. Sauté celery and 2 Tbsp. onion for 2 minutes, add mushrooms, and cook for another minute. Add to spinach, along with cottage cheese, egg, pepper, marjoram and dill weed.

In 3 Tbsp. oil, sauté remaining 1 Tbsp. onion for 3 minutes. Add flour, dry mustard and nutmeg. Add milk and heat to boiling, stirring, until thickened. Pour sauce into 9" x 13" baking dish.

Spoon cottage cheese mixture into shells, then place each shell into baking pan. Cover pan with foil and bake at 375 degrees F for 15 minutes. Remove cover, sprinkle with cheese, and bake for 10 minutes longer.

Serves 6.

— Shelley Townsend
Lethbridge, Alberta

BAKED CHEESE SHELLS
WITH GARLIC CROUTONS

2 cups large-shell vegetable macaroni
3 cups grated old Cheddar cheese
2 cups grated Gouda cheese
1¼ cups milk
½ tsp. salt
¼ tsp. pepper
¼ tsp. basil

Croutons
3 Tbsp. butter
3 cloves garlic, minced
3-4 slices whole wheat bread, cubed

Cook shells, drain, then toss with 2 cups Cheddar cheese, Gouda cheese, milk and seasonings. Pour into greased casserole dish. Sprinkle with remaining Cheddar cheese.

To make croutons, melt butter in skillet. Add garlic and brown lightly. Add cubed bread and toss. Discard garlic.

Scatter croutons over casserole, and bake at 350 degrees F for 20 to 25 minutes.

Serves 4.

— Vicki de Boer
Whaletown, British Columbia

FETA CRUNCH

½ lb. spinach, steamed & chopped
1½ cups bean sprouts
8 oz. feta cheese
¼ cup chopped walnuts
1 onion, chopped & sautéed
¾ cup raw macaroni elbows, cooked
1 egg
2 Tbsp. milk

Combine spinach, sprouts, cheese, walnuts and onion.

In greased casserole dish, place macaroni in a layer, then spoon spinach mixture over this. Beat egg and milk together, and pour over casserole. Cover and bake at 350 degrees F for 20 minutes.

Serves 2.

— Nora Galligan
Toronto, Ontario

MACARONI WITH SAUSAGE

1 lb. sausage meat
1 onion, finely chopped
1 clove garlic, chopped
¼ cup sliced mushrooms
1 Tbsp. butter
¼ tsp. savory
¼ tsp. celery seed
¼ tsp. oregano
¼ tsp. chili powder
¼ tsp. pepper
¼ tsp. dry mustard
6-oz. can tomato paste
¼ cup water
3 cups cooked macaroni
1 cup cottage cheese

Sauté sausage meat until lightly browned. Drain off fat, separate meat with fork, and set aside. Sauté onion, garlic and mushrooms in butter. Add sausage meat, savory, celery seed, oregano, chili powder, pepper and dry mustard. Stir in tomato paste and water, and mix well. Add macaroni and stir.

Arrange alternate layers of macaroni-meat mixture and cottage cheese in greased casserole dish, ending with meat on top. Bake at 350 degrees F for 25 to 30 minutes.

Serves 8.

— Ruth Anne Laverty
Listowel, Ontario

PASTITSIO

A GREEK DISH, PASTITSIO IS A MACARONI AND MEAT CASSEROLE WITH
feta cheese, topped with a custard and baked.

1 lb. ground beef
2 large onions, minced
½ lb. mushrooms, sliced
2 cups Spicy Tomato Sauce, page 96
2 large cloves garlic, crushed
½ tsp. oregano
½ tsp. basil
¼ tsp. pepper
⅛ tsp. cinnamon
8 oz. macaroni
1 egg
½ lb. feta cheese, crumbled, or ⅓ cup Parmesan cheese

Custard
¼ cup butter
¼ cup flour
2 cups milk
½ tsp. salt
⅛ tsp. pepper
⅛ tsp. nutmeg
2 eggs, beaten

Brown ground beef. Add onions and sauté until tender. Stir in mushrooms
and cook for 5 minutes. Add Spicy Tomato Sauce, garlic, oregano, basil,
pepper and cinnamon. Lower heat, cover, and simmer for 40 to 50
minutes or until thickened.

Cook macaroni, drain, and rinse in cold water. Beat egg, then mix into
macaroni. Spread half the macaroni in greased 9" x 13" baking dish. Cover
with meat sauce. Top with remaining macaroni, then sprinkle with half
the cheese. Bake at 350 degrees F for 15 minutes.

Meanwhile, prepare custard. Melt butter in saucepan, and stir in flour.
Add milk. Cook, stirring, until thick and glossy. Add spices, remove from
heat, and cool slightly. Whisk a small amount of hot sauce into eggs, then
beat egg mixture into remaining sauce.

Remove casserole from oven, cover with custard, and sprinkle with
remaining cheese. Bake 40 minutes longer, or until a knife inserted comes
out clean.

Serves 4.

— Shelley Townsend
Lethbridge, Alberta

BAKED MACARONI WITH THREE CHEESES

1 small onion, chopped
1 clove garlic, minced
3 Tbsp. butter
¼ cup chopped basil
3 Tbsp. flour
2 cups milk
Salt & pepper
¾ lb. macaroni, cooked
2 cups mixed grated Cheddar, Parmesan & Gouda cheeses
2 tomatoes, sliced

Sauté onion and garlic in butter until translucent. Add basil and sauté for a few minutes. Stir in flour and cook for 1 minute. Add milk and salt and pepper, and cook, stirring constantly, until sauce thickens.

In a greased casserole dish, layer macaroni, sauce, cheese and tomatoes, ending with cheese and tomatoes.

Bake at 350 degrees F for 30 minutes.

Serves 4.

— L. Simpson
Lethbridge, Alberta

CHICKEN WITH CASHEWS & NOODLES

SUBSTITUTING BLACK OLIVES FOR THE CELERY PROVIDES A TASTY variation of this recipe.

¼ cup oil
2 cloves garlic, minced
1 onion, chopped
1 sweet red pepper, chopped
1 cup chopped celery
1 lb. chicken breasts, diced
2 cups cream of mushroom sauce
¼ cup white wine
½ cup Parmesan cheese
½ cup sliced roasted cashews
¾ lb. broad egg noodles, cooked

Heat oil. Sauté garlic, onion, red pepper and celery for 10 minutes. Add chicken, and cook, stirring, until chicken is cooked through. Add mushroom sauce, wine, Parmesan cheese and cashews. Mix with noodles, place in greased casserole dish, and bake at 350 degrees F for 30 minutes.

Serves 4.

— L. Simpson
Lethbridge, Alberta

SAVOURY NOODLE BAKE

2 Tbsp. oil
4 Tbsp. butter
2 onions, finely chopped
1 clove garlic, minced
2 cups canned tomatoes
⅛ tsp. salt
Pepper
¼ tsp. oregano or basil
1 bay leaf
8 oz. egg noodles
3 cups grated Cheddar cheese

Combine oil and 2 Tbsp. butter, place over low heat, and when butter has melted, add onions and garlic. Cook over low heat until soft.

Combine tomatoes, salt and spices. Add to onion mixture; simmer for 15 minutes, and discard bay leaf.

Cook noodles until tender; rinse with hot water and drain. Add remaining 2 Tbsp. butter and 2 cups cheese. Add tomato sauce. Turn mixture into greased baking dish, and top with remaining 1 cup cheese.

Bake at 350 degrees F for 30 minutes.

— *Georgina Mitchell*
Bainsville, Ontario

COTTAGE CHEESE & NOODLE BAKE

½ cup chopped onion
2 Tbsp. butter
2 Tbsp. flour
1 tsp. salt
Pepper
1 cup milk
1 tsp. mustard
1 cup cottage cheese
½ cup grated Cheddar cheese
2 Tbsp. lemon juice
8 oz. medium egg noodles, cooked
Parsley

Sauté onion in butter until tender. Stir in flour, salt and pepper until smooth. Gradually stir in milk and mustard. Cook until thickened. Stir in cheeses, lemon juice, then noodles.

Pour into a greased casserole dish.

Bake at 350 degrees F for 40 to 45 minutes. Sprinkle with fresh parsley to serve.

Serves 4.

CREAMY NOODLES

8 oz. fine egg noodles
1⅔ cups fine curd cottage cheese
1⅔ cups sour cream
1 clove garlic, minced
⅔ cup chopped onion
1 Tbsp. Worcestershire sauce
2 Tbsp. sesame seeds
Salt
Parmesan cheese

Cook noodles and drain. Combine remaining ingredients, toss with noodles, and place in greased casserole dish. Refrigerate for at least 2 hours.

When ready to serve, warm to room temperature, then bake at 350 degrees F for 45 minutes. Serve with Parmesan cheese.

Serves 6.

— Valerie Gillis
Renfrew, Ontario

NUTTY NOODLE BAKE

3 Tbsp. oil
1 onion, chopped
¾ cup peanuts
½ cup cashews
6 oz. cooked, drained noodles
2 cups yogurt
½ cup tahini
½ tsp. nutmeg
Salt & pepper
¼ cup toasted sesame seed meal
Parsley

Heat oil and sauté onion. Stir in nuts, and cook until lightly browned. Add noodles, stir, and place in greased casserole dish.

Bake at 350 degrees F until heated through — about 20 minutes. Remove from oven, and stir in yogurt, tahini, nutmeg and salt and pepper. Garnish with sesame seed meal and parsley.

Serves 6.

— Helen Shepherd
Lansdowne, Ontario

PARISIENNE GNOCCHI

GNOCCHI CAN BE MADE, AS IN THIS RECIPE, FROM A PASTA-LIKE DOUGH, or from a dough based on mashed potatoes. This recipe results in a lighter, less pasty dish.

Gnocchi
2 cups milk
4½ Tbsp. butter
Salt
Nutmeg
1⅓ cups flour
5-6 eggs
6 Tbsp. Parmesan cheese

Mornay Sauce
2 Tbsp. butter
2 Tbsp. flour
2 cups milk
Salt
Nutmeg
¾ cups grated Gruyère cheese

1 Tbsp. melted butter
4 Tbsp. Parmesan cheese

Bring milk, butter, salt and nutmeg to a boil in a large pan. Pour flour in all at once, and cook mixture, stirring constantly, until it leaves the sides of the pan. Remove from heat and cool slightly. Add eggs one at a time, beating vigorously, then Parmesan cheese. Cool.

Using pastry bag fitted with large round tube, pipe dough out, cutting it off at 1-inch lengths so that dough falls into a large pot of boiling, salted water. Remove gnocchi from water as they rise to the surface. Drain.

To prepare Mornay sauce, melt butter in saucepan, stir in flour, then milk, salt and nutmeg. Remove from heat and stir in Gruyère cheese.

Pour a thin layer of Mornay sauce into casserole dish, add gnocchi, and cover with remaining sauce. Sprinkle with melted butter and Parmesan cheese.

Bake at 400 degrees F for 15 minutes or until golden.

Serves 4.

— *Dolores S.C. Greco*
Schomberg, Ontario

STOVETOPS

The saucepot is bubbling and all is well

SPICY TOMATO SAUCE

THIS IS A BASIC TOMATO SAUCE. MEAT MAY BE ADDED OR THE seasonings adjusted to suit personal taste.

4-6 Tbsp. oil
2 onions, chopped
4 cloves garlic, crushed
4 Tbsp. chopped basil
3 Tbsp. chopped oregano
½ cup chopped parsley
1 bay leaf
6 cups canned tomatoes
13-oz. can tomato paste
Salt & pepper

Heat oil. Sauté onions and garlic until translucent, then add basil, oregano, parsley and bay leaf. Cook for 2 minutes. Add tomatoes, tomato paste and salt and pepper, bring to a boil, then simmer for at least 1 hour.

Makes 8 cups.

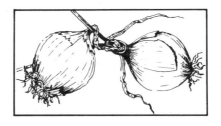

SPINACH SAUCE

¼ cup butter
10 oz. spinach, finely chopped
1 tsp. salt
1 cup cottage cheese
¼ cup Parmesan cheese
¼ cup milk
⅛ tsp. nutmeg

Melt butter, add spinach and salt, and cook until spinach is limp – about 5 minutes. Lower heat to simmer, stir in cheeses, milk and nutmeg, and cook, stirring, until mixture is heated through. Serve with cooked spaghetti.

Serves 6.

WHITE SAUCE FOR SPAGHETTI

2 Tbsp. fresh parsley
2 Tbsp. fresh basil
1 cup butter, melted
⅓ cup Parmesan cheese
¼ cup olive oil
2 cloves garlic, crushed
8 oz. cream cheese
⅔ cup boiling water

Mix together parsley, basil and butter. Add cheese, then mix in remaining ingredients. Simmer until well blended. Serve over cooked noodles.

Makes 2½ cups.

— Ken Parejko
Holcombe, Wisconsin

PESTO SAUCE

2 cups fresh basil
2 cloves garlic
½ cup parsley
½ tsp. salt
⅓-½ cup olive oil
¼ cup Parmesan cheese
3 Tbsp. pine nuts

Place basil, garlic, parsley, salt and ⅓ cup oil in blender. Process, adding more oil if necessary to make a smooth paste. Add cheese and nuts, and blend for a few seconds. Serve over hot, buttered spaghetti.

Serves 4.

TOFU TOMATO SAUCE

4 Tbsp. olive oil
3 cloves garlic, minced
1 large onion, chopped
1 green pepper, chopped
2 cups sliced mushrooms
2 zucchini, sliced
1 lb. tofu, mashed
26-oz. can tomatoes, drained
6½-oz. can tomato paste
½ cup red wine
1 cup Parmesan cheese

Heat oil in large, heavy pan. Sauté garlic, onion and green pepper until onion is translucent. Add mushrooms, zucchini, tofu, tomatoes and tomato paste. Simmer for 30 minutes, stirring frequently. Add wine and simmer for 10 more minutes, then stir in Parmesan cheese and serve over hot, buttered pasta.

Serves 6.

— L. Simpson
Lethbridge, Alberta

TOMATO CHEESE SAUCE

4 Tbsp. butter
2 cloves garlic, minced
14-oz. can crushed tomatoes
Salt & pepper
1 tsp. basil
1½ Tbsp. flour
1½ cups hot milk
1 Tbsp. brandy
¼ cup Parmesan cheese
¾ lb. penne, cooked, drained & buttered

Melt 2 Tbsp. butter, and sauté garlic. Add tomatoes, salt and pepper and basil. Simmer while preparing rest of dish.

Melt remaining 2 Tbsp. butter, and stir in flour. Cook, stirring, until thickened. Gradually add hot milk, and cook and stir until thickened. Add tomato mixture and brandy, then stir in Parmesan cheese.

Toss with penne. Serve with more Parmesan cheese if desired.

Serves 4 to 6.

— Wendy Vine
Ganges, British Columbia

RED ONION SAUCE

½ cup butter
2 bay leaves
3 cloves garlic, crushed
2½ lbs. red onions, thickly sliced
½ tsp. salt
1 cup dry red wine
¼ tsp. thyme
¼ tsp. cayenne
¼ tsp. basil
¼ tsp. oregano
½ tsp. sage
2 cups chopped tomatoes
¼ cup brandy
1 tsp. lemon juice
2 tsp. white wine vinegar
Pepper

Melt butter in large, heavy pot. Add bay leaves and garlic, and cook, stirring constantly, for 1 minute. Add onions and sauté, stirring frequently, for 30 minutes, or until the onions are lightly browned. Add salt and cook for a few minutes.

Add remaining ingredients, lower heat, and simmer, stirring occasionally, for about 1 hour, or until sauce is thick.

Serves 6.

— *Holly Andrews*
Puslinch, Ontario

SUNFLOWER SPAGHETTI SAUCE

THIS VEGETARIAN SPAGHETTI SAUCE CAN BE SERVED OVER ANY NUMBER of pastas — rotini, linguine, spaghetti or mostaccioli, to mention a few.

2½ cups Spicy Tomato Sauce, page 96
1 tsp. oregano
1 clove garlic, crushed
½ tsp. cumin
1 bay leaf
½ cup ground sunflower seeds
½ cup sunflower seeds

Combine all ingredients, and simmer for 30 minutes, stirring occasionally. Serve over pasta, and top with Parmesan cheese.

Serves 6.

— *Helen Shepherd*
Lansdowne, Ontario

CREAMY GARLIC SAUCE

THE CREAMINESS OF THIS SAUCE COMPLEMENTS ITS TANGY GARLIC
flavour — cottage cheese may be substituted if ricotta is unavailable.

½ cup milk
2 Tbsp. butter
3-4 cloves garlic, crushed
1 lb. ricotta cheese
Pasta of your choice, cooked
½ cup Parmesan cheese
Pepper

Heat milk and butter in heavy pot. Add garlic and simmer for 5 minutes,
then remove garlic. Add ricotta cheese and cook, stirring, over low heat
until ricotta has melted. Remove from heat and cover.

Drain pasta, toss with ricotta mixture, and add Parmesan cheese and
pepper.

Serves 2 or 3.

— Irene Louden
Port Coquitlam, British Columbia

CREAMY PASTA SAUCE WITH FRESH TARRAGON

1 cup packed fresh tarragon leaves
2-4 cloves garlic
1 Tbsp. green peppercorns
½ cup bread crumbs
1 Tbsp. fresh lemon juice
1 cup pine nuts
½ cup olive oil
¼ cup water

Mix tarragon and garlic into a paste in blender or food processor. Add
peppercorns, bread crumbs and lemon juice, and blend until smooth. Add
nuts, processing until smooth. Pour in oil, then water in a slow stream and
blend. Mixture should be thick and creamy.

Serve at room temperature over hot, buttered pasta.

Makes 2 cups.

— Noel Richardson
Saanichton, British Columbia

FRESH HERB SAUCE SUPREME WITH PASTA

ANY OF TARRAGON, BASIL, FENNEL (THIS RESULTS IN A PLEASANT LICORICE taste), chervil or chives can be used here — or a combination of two or more.

4 Tbsp. butter
1½ cups whipping cream
½ tsp. nutmeg
4 cups hot, cooked fettuccine
1 egg yolk
1 cup Parmesan cheese
½ cup finely chopped fresh herbs

Melt butter, and add cream and nutmeg. Stir in pasta and cook for 2 minutes. Add egg yolk, stirring well.

Remove from heat, and stir in ¾ cup of the cheese and the herbs. Serve immediately, topped with the remaining cheese.

Serves 4.

— Noel Richardson
Saanichton, British Columbia

ZUCCHINI GARLIC SAUCE

QUICK AND EASY TO PREPARE, THIS SPAGHETTI SAUCE SHOULD BE A staple in the diet of any family with a zucchini patch in the garden.

3 Tbsp. oil
6-10 cloves garlic, crushed
3-4 zucchini, diced
½ tsp. basil
½ tsp. oregano
½ tsp. thyme
Salt & pepper
Parmesan cheese

Heat oil in heavy pot. Add garlic and zucchini. After a few minutes, sprinkle with herbs, cover, and simmer, stirring occasionally, until zucchini is soft and pulpy — 15 to 20 minutes.

Serve over spaghettini, and top with Parmesan cheese.

Serves 3 to 4.

— Anne Levesque
Inverness, Nova Scotia

ARTICHOKE HEART SAUCE FOR SPAGHETTI

THIS IS A VERY SPICY TOPPING, PARTICULARLY GOOD WITH FRESH fettuccine. Served as an appetizer, it provides a tangy beginning to a meal.

1 large can artichoke hearts, sliced
½ cup olive oil
1 tsp. crushed hot red pepper
1 tsp. salt
3 cloves garlic, minced
4 Tbsp. chopped parsley
Juice of 1 lemon
Pepper
Parmesan cheese

Combine artichoke hearts, oil, red pepper, salt and garlic in heavy pot. Cook, stirring, until hot. Add parsley and lemon juice. Serve over cooked noodles, topped with pepper and Parmesan cheese.

Serves 4.

LEMON PASTA SAUCE

WHEN SERVING LINGUINE AS AN ACCOMPANIMENT TO VEAL SCALLOPINE, sole almandine or a similar dish, this delicate sauce is a perfect topping.

½ cup butter
½ cup flour
3 Tbsp. sugar
1 tsp. salt
4 cups water
1 cup lemon juice
1 lb. linguine, cooked & drained

Melt butter, add flour, sugar and salt, and stir to make a roux. Cook for 2 minutes, then add water and lemon juice, and cook until thickened.

Pour over linguine, toss, and serve.

Serves 12 as an accompaniment.

— *Edna Craig*
Edmonton, Alberta

FETTUCCINE ALFREDO

THIS RICH PASTA DISH IS PARTICULARLY DELICIOUS SERVED WITH VEAL cooked in a cream sauce or with stuffed zucchini. If spinach noodles are used, the dish will be an attractive green.

½ lb. fettuccine
¼ lb. butter
1 cup whipping cream
½ cup Parmesan cheese
½ cup chopped parsley
Salt & pepper

Cook noodles in boiling, salted water. Drain. Return to pot. Over low heat, stir in butter, cream and cheese, and cook, mixing well, until butter is melted and mixture is hot. Stir in parsley and salt and pepper.

Serves 2 as a main dish, 4 as a side dish.

BOUNTIFUL PASTA

1 lb. spaghetti
¼ cup butter
2 Tbsp. vegetable oil
1½ cups whole cherry tomatoes
1 clove garlic, minced
¼ cup chopped green onion
½ tsp. salt
1 tsp. basil
5 cups broccoli, cut into bite-sized pieces
½ cup coarsely chopped walnuts
1 cup chicken stock
½ cup Parmesan cheese
2-4 Tbsp. parsley

Boil spaghetti, drain, and set aside.

Melt half the butter in a skillet, and pour in oil. Add tomatoes and sauté for 5 minutes until tender. Stir in garlic, onion, salt and basil, and cook for 2 more minutes. Set aside and keep warm.

Meanwhile, steam broccoli until tender. Toast walnuts for 5 minutes and set aside.

Melt remaining butter in a saucepan. Add stock, cheese and parsley, and mix well. Add tomatoes, broccoli and spaghetti, and toss. Pour onto a warm platter and sprinkle with nuts.

Serves 4.

— *Pat Dicer*
Mission, British Columbia

PASTA PRIMAVERA

AFTER TASTING THIS DISH, THE CONTRIBUTOR'S SISTER-IN-LAW, A
hospital nutritionist, incorporated it into the hospital staff's menu with
great success.

2 heads broccoli
4 small zucchini
1 lb. asparagus
1 lb. linguine
1 clove garlic, chopped
2 pints cherry tomatoes, stemmed & halved
¼ cup oil
¼ cup chopped fresh basil
1 lb. mushrooms, thinly sliced
½ cup peas
¼ cup chopped fresh parsley
1½ tsp. salt
¼ tsp. pepper
¼ tsp. crushed red pepper
¼ cup butter
¾ cup heavy cream
⅔ cup Parmesan cheese

Wash broccoli, zucchini and asparagus. Cut broccoli into bite-sized pieces,
zucchini into thin slices, and asparagus into 1-inch pieces. Cook in boiling
water until tender-crisp, drain, and place in large bowl.

Cook, drain, and rinse linguine.

Sauté garlic and tomatoes in oil in large skillet for 2 minutes. Stir in basil
and mushrooms, and cook for 3 minutes. Stir in peas, parsley, salt, pepper
and red pepper. Cook for 1 minute. Add to vegetables in bowl.

Melt butter and stir in cream and cheese. Cook over medium heat, stirring
constantly, until smooth. Add linguine and toss to coat. Stir in vegetables,
and cook gently until heated through.

Serves 6.

— Christine Taylor
Norbertville, Quebec

LINGUINE WITH ZUCCHINI AL PESTO

2 small zucchini, cut into strips
2 Tbsp. butter
½ cup fresh basil
½ cup snipped parsley
3 cloves garlic, crushed
4 Tbsp. pine nuts, lightly roasted
Handful Parmesan cheese
1 cup olive oil
6 Tbsp. butter, softened
8 oz. linguine
Salt & pepper

Fry zucchini in butter until limp and golden. Whir in blender basil, parsley, garlic, pine nuts and Parmesan cheese, adding oil and butter a little at a time to keep the sauce thick.

Cook linguine until just tender. Combine linguine, zucchini and sauce. Add salt and pepper to taste.

Serves 4 to 6.

— *Cary Elizabeth Marshall*
Thunder Bay, Ontario

EGGPLANT & FETA WITH NOODLES

2 cloves garlic, minced
1 onion, chopped
2 Tbsp. olive oil
1 large eggplant, chopped
1 lb. mushrooms, sliced
½ cup sliced black olives
5 large tomatoes, peeled & chopped
1 tsp. basil
Salt & pepper
1 cup crumbled feta cheese
¾ lb. fettuccine, cooked & drained

Sauté garlic and onion in oil until onion is translucent. Add eggplant, mushrooms and olives, and simmer, stirring occasionally, for 20 minutes. Add tomatoes, basil and salt and pepper, and simmer for another 20 minutes. Add feta cheese.

Toss with fettuccine and serve.

Serves 4 to 6.

— *L. Simpson*
Lethbridge, Alberta

SPAGHETTI WITH FRESH TOMATOES & THREE CHEESES

½ lb. zite
3 Tbsp. butter
2 eggs, slightly beaten
1 large clove garlic, crushed
3 Tbsp. chopped basil
1 cup grated muenster cheese
½ cup provolone cheese
½ cup Romano cheese
½ cup chopped parsley
6 tomatoes, sliced

Cook zite, drain, and return to pot over low heat. Toss with butter, eggs, garlic, basil and muenster cheese. Stir gently until cheese begins to melt. Stir in provolone and Romano cheeses. Place in serving dish, and top with parsley and tomatoes.

Serves 4.

— Shelley Townsend
Lethbridge, Alberta

NOODLE OMELETTE

2 Tbsp. butter
1 Tbsp. oil
1 cup chopped onion
1 green pepper, sliced into strips
1 cup grated Swiss cheese
8 eggs, beaten
2½ cups cooked noodles
1 tsp. salt

Melt 1 Tbsp. butter and oil in a heavy skillet. Sauté onion and green pepper until onion browns. Stir in remaining butter, and reduce heat to very low.

Combine remaining ingredients and pour over vegetables. Cover and cook over medium-low heat, without stirring, for 15 to 20 minutes. When puffed and browned around the edges, the omelette is cooked.

Serves 8.

SPAGHETTI BELLINI

THIS IS ONE OF SICILY'S BEST-KNOWN EGGPLANT AND PASTA DISHES.
The ricotta salata called for is a dry ricotta made from sheep's milk.

12 ripe tomatoes
Salt
1 lb. ricotta salata
4 small eggplants
4 cups olive oil
2 cups coarsely chopped basil
¾ lb. spaghetti

Halve tomatoes, salt heavily, and let drain overnight. Squeeze, saving pulp
and juice. Chop pulp. Heat juice, reducing to a thick liquid, add pulp and
cook for just a few minutes.

Bake ricotta at 375 degrees F for 30 minutes. Let cool.

Cut a checkerboard pattern in the eggplants, going deep but not through to
the skin on the other side. Heat oil to 375 degrees F, and plunge eggplants
into it. Fry until done — the cuts will open up into a beautiful grid.

Meanwhile, cook pasta. The eggplants get mushy if they have to sit after
being cooked, so timing is important.

To serve, toss tomato sauce and basil with spaghetti. Grate ricotta over
this, then place the eggplant, which has been salted, grid side up, on top of
everything.

Serves 4.

BASIL BUTTER BALLS

SIMPLE IT IS, BUT SEASONED, BUTTERED PASTA IS ONE OF THE MOST
delicious treats possible. These butter balls can be assembled and stored in
the freezer, removed at the last minute and served with cooked fresh
pasta for a quick and easy supper. A tossed salad is all that is needed to
complete this meal.

½ cup unsalted butter
10 basil leaves
1 clove garlic
¼ tsp. pepper

In blender or food processor, purée ingredients. Shape into small balls,
place on cookie sheet and freeze. When balls are well frozen, remove from
cookie sheet and store in covered container in freezer. To serve, remove
from freezer, warm to room temperature, and serve on hot pasta.

— Louise McDonald
L'Orignal, Ontario

PASTA E PISELLI

THIS IS A SOUTHERN ITALIAN RECIPE FOR PASTA WITH PEAS, WHICH HAS been in the contributor's family for four generations.

2 cloves garlic
⅓ cup olive oil
1 medium onion, sliced
1 lb. tomatoes, coarsely chopped
½ lb. fresh peas
½ tsp. oregano
Salt & pepper
Chili pepper flakes
1 lb. bite-sized pasta
2 eggs
½ cup Parmesan or Romano cheese
2 Tbsp. milk

Peel garlic and brown in oil in large skillet, then remove garlic and discard. Sauté onion in oil until tender. Add tomatoes, peas, oregano, salt and pepper and chili pepper. Cover and simmer slowly as pasta cooks.

Cook pasta in boiling, salted water. While pasta is cooking, beat eggs in bowl and mix in cheese and milk.

Drain cooked pasta and return to pot. Add vegetable mixture, then egg-cheese mixture, and heat slowly, stirring constantly, until eggs are cooked.

Serves 6.

— Anthony Balzano
Piscataway, New Jersey

BUTTERED WALNUT NOODLES

½ lb. broad egg noodles
3 Tbsp. butter
¼ cup chopped walnuts
1 tsp. salt
½ tsp. paprika

Crush approximately 1 cup raw noodles to make ¼ cup crushed noodles.

Melt butter in small saucepan. Stir in crushed noodles, and cook until lightly browned. Add walnuts, and cook over low heat, stirring constantly, until noodles and nuts are golden. Stir in salt and paprika.

Cook remaining noodles and drain. Return to saucepan. Toss with noodle-nut mixture and serve immediately.

Serves 4.

— Pam Collacott
North Gower, Ontario

CRISPY NOODLES WITH STIR-FRIED BROCCOLI

WHEN FRIED AFTER BEING BOILED, THE STRANDS OF VERMICELLI STICK together to form a pancake.

1 lb. vermicelli
4 Tbsp. oil
1 head broccoli, broken into florets
2 cloves garlic, minced
1 onion, thinly sliced
1 lb. tofu, diced
1¾ cups vegetable stock
3-4 Tbsp. soya sauce
1 Tbsp. cornstarch
1 tsp. ginger

Cook vermicelli until tender, and drain well. Heat 2 Tbsp. oil in wok and add noodles. Cook over medium-high heat until bottom is golden, then flip over, and cook other side. Remove from wok and keep warm.

Add remaining 2 Tbsp. oil. Stir-fry broccoli, garlic, onion and tofu until tender-crisp.

Meanwhile, combine stock, soya sauce, cornstarch and ginger. Stir into vegetables, and cook until sauce thickens and clears.

To serve, cut noodle pancake in wedges and ladle broccoli-tofu mixture on top.

Serves 4.

— Anne Levesque
Inverness, Nova Scotia

SPAGHETTI WITH GARLIC & OIL

QUICK AND SIMPLE, THIS DISH ALLOWS THE DINER TO REALLY APPRECIATE the flavours of the pasta and the garlic.

4 oz. spaghetti
½ cup olive oil
4 cloves garlic, peeled & crushed
Pepper

Cook spaghetti in boiling, salted water. When almost cooked, heat oil in heavy pot. Add garlic and cook until browned. Drain and rinse spaghetti. Mix with garlic-oil mixture and serve topped with pepper.

Serves 2.

AGLIO OGLIO ESTATE

THE CONTRIBUTOR OBTAINED THIS RECIPE FROM AN ELDERLY SICILIAN
woman when he was searching for a garlicky sauce that he could make
before his fresh garlic was ready. It is a variation of the traditional pesto
sauce.

1 cup coarsely chopped garlic shoots
½ cup olive oil
2 Tbsp. pine nuts
Salt
½ cup Parmesan cheese
2 Tbsp. Romano cheese

Combine garlic shoots, oil, nuts and salt in a blender or food processor,
and blend into a paste.

Pour into a bowl and beat in cheeses by hand. Pour over hot, buttered
pasta and serve.

Serves 4.

— *Michael Pray*
Hamilton, Ontario

FRIED PASTA

THIS IS AN EXCELLENT WAY TO USE UP LEFTOVER PASTA — IF THAT
situation should ever arise! Of course, freshly cooked pasta, usually
spaghetti, fettuccine or some other strand-type noodle, can also be used.

3 cups cooked pasta
2-3 Tbsp. butter
Salt & pepper
Chopped parsley

Sauté pasta in butter until golden and slightly crispy, adding butter if
necessary. Season and serve.

Serves 2.

— *Mara Smelters Wier*
Toronto, Ontario

PASTA TUTTO MARE

4 Tbsp. butter
3¾ cups light cream
1½ cups sliced mushrooms
¼ lb. mild semisoft cheese (e.g. mozzarella or brick), cubed
1 Tbsp. finely chopped parsley
1 tsp. minced garlic
1 tsp. salt
Curry
Pepper
8 oz. cooked crabmeat
8 oz. cooked shrimp
1 lb. small pasta shells
1½ cups Parmesan cheese

Melt butter in heavy skillet. Add cream, mushrooms, cheese, parsley, garlic, salt, curry and pepper. Bring to a boil over medium heat, stirring constantly. Add crabmeat, shrimp and pasta, sprinkle with Parmesan cheese, and reduce heat to low. Simmer, uncovered, stirring frequently, until slightly thickened — 2 to 3 minutes.

Serves 4 to 6.

— Lucia Cyre
Logan Lake, British Columbia

NOODLES WITH SOUR CREAM

1 lb. medium egg noodles
2 Tbsp. butter
2 cups sour cream
½ tsp. salt
Cayenne
3 Tbsp. fresh chopped chives
1 clove garlic, minced
¼ cup Parmesan cheese

Cook noodles until tender, drain, and return to pot. Toss with remaining ingredients and serve immediately.

Serves 6 to 8.

— Helen Shepherd
Lansdowne, Ontario

POPPY SEED NOODLES

½ lb. broad egg noodles
¼ cup poppy seeds
3 Tbsp. melted butter
1 tsp. lemon juice
1 tsp. chopped parsley
Salt & pepper

Cook noodles until tender and drain. Combine poppy seeds and butter, and add to hot noodles with remaining ingredients. Mix lightly and serve.

Serves 2.

— Mikell Billoki
Gore Bay, Ontario

SPINACH LINGUINE WITH RED CLAM SAUCE

FRESH PASTA, EASILY MADE AT HOME AND INCREASINGLY AVAILABLE IN specialty stores, offers a flavour and texture that is far superior to commercial dried noodles. The pasta becomes an integral part of the dish, not just the base for the sauce. Fresh pasta, with a cooking time of less than 5 minutes, is strongly recommended for this recipe.

2 Tbsp. olive oil
2 cloves garlic, minced
1 small onion, chopped
1 tsp. chopped fresh marjoram
1 tsp. chopped fresh basil
3 tomatoes, peeled & chopped
1 Tbsp. tomato paste
4 Tbsp. dry white wine
10-oz. can baby clams
½ lb. spinach linguine
Parmesan cheese

Heat olive oil in heavy pot, and sauté garlic and onion for 5 minutes. Add marjoram and basil, and sauté for 2 more minutes. Stir in tomatoes, tomato paste, wine and clams; cover and simmer for 20 minutes.

Cook linguine until just tender. Drain, rinse under hot water, and serve immediately with clam sauce. Top with Parmesan cheese.

Serves 4.

— Jane Pugh
Toronto, Ontario

Fried Jao-Tze, page 47

Cappellettini in Brodo, page 50

Pasta Salad Niçoise, page 58

Artichoke Heart Sauce for Spaghetti, page 102

Ravioli, page 126

Spaghetti with Spicy Tomato Sauce, page 96, and Uncle Al's Meatballs, page 133

Fiocchi, page 143

Kugel, page 146

LINGUINE WITH MUSHROOM & CLAM SAUCE

EITHER REGULAR OR SPINACH LINGUINE CAN BE USED IN THIS RECIPE.

8 oz. linguine
1 Tbsp. butter
2 cups sliced mushrooms
¼ cup sliced green onions
2 cloves garlic, minced
½ cup light cream
¼ cup white wine
12-oz. can clams, drained
2 Tbsp. chopped parsley
2 Tbsp. Parmesan cheese

Cook linguine until just tender, drain and rinse. Heat butter in large skillet, and sauté mushrooms, onions and garlic until tender. Add cream and wine, and simmer for 1 minute. Add clams and parsley, and simmer for 3 minutes more.

Pour sauce over linguine and toss. Sprinkle with Parmesan cheese and serve.

Serves 4.

— *Cinda Chavich*
Saskatoon, Saskatchewan

CLAM SAUCE FOR SPAGHETTI

¼ cup butter
5 cloves garlic, peeled & halved
2 Tbsp. whole wheat flour
2 Tbsp. powdered milk
10-oz. can whole baby butter clams
Oregano
6 oz. spaghetti, cooked

Melt butter and slowly sauté garlic for 3 minutes. Do not let butter brown. Remove garlic and add flour and milk. Blend well and remove from heat.

Drain clams and add liquid to flour slowly, beating well with a whisk. Return sauce to medium heat, and cook for about 4 minutes or until thick. Add clams and oregano, and pour over spaghetti.

Serves 2.

— *Linda Townsend*
Nanaimo, British Columbia

CUCUMBER CLAM SPAGHETTI SAUCE

4 Tbsp. olive oil
1 clove garlic, peeled
10-oz. can clams, with juice reserved
2 seedless cucumbers, sliced
1 tsp. salt
Pepper
1 Tbsp. chopped parsley
8 oz. spaghetti, cooked

Heat oil and sauté garlic until browned, then discard. Drain clam juice into pan, stir in cucumbers, salt and pepper. Cook, uncovered, stirring occasionally, for about 15 minutes. Add clams and cook gently for 5 more minutes. Stir in parsley and cook 1 minute further. Serve over cooked spaghetti.

Serves 4.

— Judith Goodwin
Tamworth, Ontario

VICKI'S BIRTHDAY SHRIMP

2 cloves garlic, minced
2 Tbsp. olive oil
½ cup white wine
1 Tbsp. basil
24 large shrimp, cleaned & shelled
1 zucchini, sliced
¼ lb. snow peas
½ lb. mushrooms
1 green pepper, sliced
½ red pepper, sliced
2 cups peeled, chopped fresh tomatoes
1-2 Tbsp. flour
8 oz. fettuccine, cooked, drained, rinsed & buttered

Combine garlic, olive oil, wine and basil. Marinate shrimp in this for several hours.

Stir-fry zucchini, snow peas, mushrooms and peppers until crispy-tender. Remove from pan.

Place shrimp and marinade in pan, and cook briefly until shrimp are firm and pink. Remove shrimp with slotted spoon. Sprinkle tomatoes with flour and add to pan. Cook until thickened, add vegetables and shrimp, and heat through. Serve over fettuccine.

Serves 4.

LINGUINE WITH SHRIMP & GREEN PEPPER

3-4 Tbsp. oil
1-2 cloves garlic, minced
1 red onion, thinly sliced
1 green pepper, thinly sliced
Salt & pepper
Chili powder
Basil
1 cup cooked shrimp
1 tomato, chopped
2 Tbsp. parsley, finely chopped
¼ cup white wine
⅛ cup brandy
1 Tbsp. butter
8 oz. linguine
Parmesan cheese

Heat oil, add garlic, onion and green pepper, and sauté until golden
brown. Add salt and pepper, chili powder, basil, shrimp, tomato and
parsley. Simmer for 7 minutes. Add wine and brandy and flame briefly.
Add butter and simmer for 5 minutes.

Meanwhile, cook linguine, drain, and add to skillet. Mix well and sprinkle
with cheese.

Serves 4.

— *Anna Sarraino*
Weston, Ontario

GREENLANDIC SHRIMP FETTUCCINE

¾ lb. fettuccine
1 bunch broccoli, broken into bite-sized pieces
¾ cup butter
1 clove garlic, crushed
1 onion, chopped
½ lb. mushrooms, sliced
1 tsp. cornstarch
1 cup cream
1¼ cups Parmesan cheese
2 lbs. Greenland shrimp, cooked & shelled

Cook fettuccine and broccoli separately until just tender. Drain and set aside.

Melt 4 Tbsp. of the butter, and sauté garlic, onion and mushrooms until tender. Remove from pan and set aside. Melt remaining butter, stir in cornstarch, then cream and cheese. Cook, stirring, until hot and thickened.

Toss together fettuccine, broccoli, onion, mushrooms, sauce and shrimp, and heat through.

Serves 6.

— *Wendy Dodd*
Frobisher Bay, Northwest Territories

CALAMARI LINGUINE

CALAMARI (DERIVED FROM THE LATIN WORD FOR PEN) ARE PEN-SHAPED squid about 6 inches in length. They should be cleaned and left to develop texture and flavour for 12 hours before cooking.

1 Tbsp. olive oil
1 large onion, sliced
6 cloves garlic, minced
1½ lbs. calamari, cut into bite-sized pieces
2 cups canned tomatoes
2 tsp. salt
¼ tsp. pepper
Tabasco sauce
¼ tsp. oregano
⅛ tsp. basil
8 oz. hot cooked linguine
2 Tbsp. chopped parsley

Heat oil and sauté onion and garlic until tender. Add calamari and cook, stirring, until no longer moist. Add tomatoes, salt, pepper, Tabasco sauce, oregano and basil, and simmer for 1 hour.

Pour sauce over linguine, garnish with parsley and serve.

Serves 4.

— Heather Quiney
Victoria, British Columbia

FETTUCCINE WITH SMOKED SALMON

THE CONTRIBUTOR OF THIS RECIPE MAKES HER OWN PASTA, AND HER husband catches and smokes the salmon. Commercial ingredients can, however, be used successfully.

2 cups light cream
Salt & pepper
1 lb. fresh fettuccine
½ lb. smoked salmon, cut into small pieces
¼ cup Parmesan cheese
Parsley

Heat cream in double boiler or heavy pot, and season with salt and pepper.

Cook fettuccine until just tender and drain. Add to warm cream, toss, then add salmon. Sprinkle with Parmesan cheese and parsley and serve.

Serves 4.

— Audrey Alley
Victoria, British Columbia

RAVIOLI

THERE ARE UNDOUBTEDLY AS MANY VARIATIONS OF BASIC RAVIOLI AS there are cooks. Here we provide two possible fillings and two suggested sauces. These may be used in any combination. The cook may even wish to make all up at once and allow guests to choose their own mixtures. Leftover fillings and sauces may be frozen for later use.

5-6 cups Basic Pasta Dough, page 23

Spinach Filling
10-oz. pkg. spinach
2 Tbsp. chopped onion
2 Tbsp. butter
1 egg, beaten
¼ cup Parmesan cheese
½ tsp. grated nutmeg

Three-Meat Filling
½ cup ground veal
½ cup ground pork
½ cup ground beef
4 Tbsp. Parmesan cheese
1 egg, beaten
Salt & pepper
1 Tbsp. chopped oregano
2 tsp. chopped sage
1 Tbsp. chopped parsley
1 tsp. chopped basil

Mushroom & Cheese Sauce
2½ Tbsp. chopped onion
4 Tbsp. butter
½ lb. mushrooms, sliced
3½ Tbsp. flour
1¼ cups milk, heated
1 cup whipping cream, heated
½ cup grated Gruyère cheese
½ cup Parmesan cheese
¾ tsp. salt
Pepper

Tomato Sauce
4-6 cups Spicy Tomato Sauce, page 96

Prepare dough and let rest, covered, while assembling fillings and sauce.

For spinach filling, cook spinach, drain, and press out all excess water. Sauté onion in butter until tender. Combine all ingredients and mix well. Set aside.

For meat filling, combine all ingredients, mixing well, and set aside.

To make cheese and mushroom sauce, sauté onions in butter until soft. Add mushrooms and cook for 10 minutes, stirring frequently. Blend in flour, milk and cream, stirring constantly, until sauce is smooth and thick. Add cheeses, season with salt and pepper, and stir until blended. Remove from heat.

Prepare Spicy Tomato Sauce and let simmer.

To assemble, put half the dough through a pasta roller to the second thinnest setting, or roll out by hand until very thin, but not paper thin. Cut into large (18" x 12") rectangles. Lightly mark rectangle into 2-inch squares with a knife or a ravioli rolling pin. Place a teaspoonful of desired filling in each square. Top with another rectangle of dough. Roll over this with ravioli rolling pin to seal edges and cut. If working by hand, press down firmly between squares, making sure dough is sealed all around the filling (it may be necessary to moisten the dough with water), then cut with a sharp knife or fluted pastry cutter.

Repeat with remaining pasta.

Heat sauces while cooking ravioli. Cook in gently simmering water for 10 to 12 minutes. Drain, and serve with butter and one or both of the sauces.

Serves 6 to 8.

— Jaine Fraser
Rockport, Massachusetts

FETTUCCINE DIJON

8 oz. fettuccine
1 cup yogurt
1 tsp. Dijon mustard
¾ cup Parmesan cheese
¾ lb. ham, cut into thin strips
2 cups chopped broccoli, cooked until tender-crisp
½ cup finely chopped green onions

Cook fettuccine in boiling, salted water until just tender. Meanwhile, place yogurt and mustard in heavy pan and whisk to blend. Heat over medium-low heat, stirring, until just warm. Stir in Parmesan cheese until it begins to melt. Add ham, broccoli and green onions. Remove from heat and cover to keep warm.

Drain and rinse fettuccine. Toss with sauce and serve immediately.

Serves 4.

— Shelley Townsend
Lethbridge, Alberta

TORTELLINI

FORMING THE TORTELLINI (SEE PAGE 38) IS A TIME-CONSUMING TASK, BUT is one that can be done ahead of time or shared with dinner guests.

1 recipe Basic Pasta Dough, page 23

Filling
1 chicken breast
½ lb. spinach
1 egg, lightly beaten
1 Tbsp. whipping cream
2 Tbsp. Parmesan cheese
Salt & pepper

Sauce
½ pint whipping cream
4 Tbsp. Parmesan cheese
¼ lb. mushrooms
1 Tbsp. chopped parsley

Prepare dough and let rest, covered, while preparing filling.

Poach chicken until tender — 10 to 15 minutes. Remove skin and bones, and chop meat finely. Steam spinach until limp and chop finely. Combine chicken, spinach, egg, cream, cheese and salt and pepper, mixing well.

Roll dough as thinly as possible by hand, or put through pasta machine to second thinnest setting. Cut into 2-inch rounds. Keep dough covered with damp cloth while working to prevent it from drying out.

Place half a teaspoon of filling in centre of each round, and form into tortellini as explained and illustrated on page 38.

Cook, without crowding, in boiling water for 10 minutes or until tender. Remove from pot, drain, and place on serving dish.

To make sauce, gently heat cream and Parmesan cheese for 2 minutes. Add mushrooms and cook for 1 more minute. Pour over tortellini, garnish with parsley and serve.

Serves 6 to 8.

— *Vivien Hoyt*
Rockwood, Ontario

SPAGHETTI CARBONARA

ACCOMPANIED BY SPINACH SALAD AND HOT CRUSTY BREAD, THIS DISH can be ready in just 30 minutes.

¼ lb. bacon, diced
2 tsp. olive oil
2 tsp. butter
1 clove garlic, minced
2 cups julienned cooked ham
8 oz. vermicelli, cooked
½ cup Parmesan or Romano cheese
¼ cup chopped parsley
Pepper
3 eggs, beaten
¼ cup sliced black olives

Brown bacon in heavy skillet until cooked but not crisp. Pour off fat and set bacon aside.

Add oil, butter, garlic and ham to same pan, and sauté over medium heat. Add vermicelli, cheese, half the parsley and the pepper. Stir to mix, then turn off heat. Pour eggs over, then toss quickly to coat spaghetti evenly. Toss in bacon and olives.

Serve immediately, garnishing with remaining parsley.

Serves 4 to 6.

NOODLES WITH ASPARAGUS & BACON

THIS MAKES A DELICIOUS LIGHT APPETIZER IN THE SPRINGTIME WHEN THE asparagus can be picked from the garden.

6 oz. fettuccine
8 thick slices bacon
4 Tbsp. unsalted butter
24 spears asparagus
Lemon slices

Cook fettuccine in boiling water until just tender. If using fresh pasta, do not cook until final step, as cooking time is so short.

As fettuccine is cooking, cut bacon into small pieces, and cook in butter until almost crisp. Keep warm. Cook asparagus until tender-crisp.

Arrange noodles on serving dish, making a well in the centre. Place asparagus in well, and spoon bacon and drippings over noodles and asparagus. Garnish with lemon slices.

Serves 4.

— Reg Manuel
Sydenham, Ontario

CHICKEN & VEGETABLE SAUCE FOR MACARONI

1 Tbsp. cornstarch
½ tsp. salt
Pepper
2 Tbsp. soya sauce
½ cup chicken stock
2 Tbsp. vegetable oil
1 clove garlic, peeled
½ lb. chicken, cut into strips
1 medium onion, sliced
1 cup sliced celery
1 cup sliced mushrooms
2 cups broccoli, cut into florets & steamed until tender-crisp
1 tomato, cut into 8 pieces
2 green onions, chopped

Combine cornstarch, salt, pepper, soya sauce and chicken stock.

Heat oil in wok or heavy skillet. Sauté garlic until golden, then discard. Add chicken and sauté for 3 or 4 minutes, stirring constantly. Remove and set aside. Add onion, celery, mushrooms and broccoli, and sauté until celery is tender – about 4 minutes. Add chicken, tomato, green onions and cornstarch mixture. Cook until thickened, stirring constantly. Serve over cooked macaroni.

Serves 4.

EGG NOODLES IN SAUCE WITH SAUSAGE

4-6 Italian sausages, cut into 2-inch lengths
2 cups uncooked egg noodles
1 onion, chopped
7 Tbsp. butter
2 cups chopped mushrooms
1 Tbsp. flour
1 cup beef stock

Brown sausages slowly in heavy pan, drain, and set aside.

Cook noodles, drain, rinse, and set aside.

Cook onion in 3 Tbsp. butter until limp and golden. Add mushrooms and 3 Tbsp. butter, and cook until mushrooms are just tender. Set aside.

Melt remaining 1 Tbsp. butter in heavy pot, add flour, and cook for 1 to 2 minutes. Add stock, and cook for 5 to 6 minutes. Add mushrooms, onions, sausages and noodles. Heat through and serve.

Serves 4.

— Suzanne Fleury
Lower Sackville, Nova Scotia

SPAGHETTI WITH LEEK & SAUSAGE SAUCE

THE AMOUNT OF HORSERADISH IN THIS RECIPE CAN BE INCREASED depending on one's taste — the amount listed below results in a mild flavour.

4 large leeks
2 cups chicken stock
Salt
5 Tbsp. butter
¼ onion, finely chopped
1 tsp. minced garlic
5 Tbsp. flour
Pepper
Cayenne
⅛ tsp. nutmeg
1 cup whipping cream
⅓-½ cup freshly grated horseradish
¾ lb. spicy Italian sausage, sliced, cooked & drained

Trim ends off leeks, cut in half lengthwise, and rinse well. Cut crosswise into 1-inch pieces. Place in saucepan with chicken stock and enough water to cover them. Add salt to taste, and boil until just tender — about 5 minutes. Drain, reserving cooking liquid.

Melt butter and briefly sauté onion and garlic. Add flour and mix well. Add cooking liquid. Cook, stirring, until thickened. Add salt, pepper, cayenne, nutmeg and cream, and bring to a boil. Add leeks, horseradish and sausage, and heat through. Serve over hot, buttered spaghetti.

Serves 6.

— Heather Quiney
Victoria, British Columbia

SAUSAGE SAUCE

EITHER MILD OR SPICY ITALIAN SAUSAGE MAY BE USED IN THE
preparation of this sauce, depending on personal taste — the contributor
uses homemade sausage from ground pork shoulder.

1 lb. Italian sausage
1 large onion, chopped
1 large stalk celery, chopped
½ green pepper, chopped
6 mushrooms, sliced
2 cloves garlic, minced
3 Tbsp. chopped fresh parsley
8 cups canned tomatoes
1 bay leaf
Salt & pepper

Brown sausage in heavy skillet. Remove from pan, drain, cut into 1-inch
slices, and return to pan with onion, celery, green pepper, mushrooms,
garlic and parsley. Sauté for a few minutes, then add tomatoes, bay leaf and
salt and pepper. Cover and simmer for 1 hour. Remove cover and simmer
for another hour or until slightly thickened.

Serve over any pasta.

Serves 4.

— Mikell Billoki
Gore Bay, Ontario

MARSALA LIVER SAUCE FOR PASTA

1 small onion, minced
¼ cup minced parsley
¼ lb. bacon, minced
½ lb. rabbit or chicken livers, quartered
¼ lb. mushrooms, thinly sliced
¼ cup Marsala wine
½ cup tomato paste
½ tsp. ground sage
Salt & pepper

Chop together onion, parsley and bacon to make a paste. Cook for 5
minutes. Add livers and mushrooms, and continue cooking until livers are
browned.

Add wine, tomato paste and seasonings, and simmer for 30 minutes. Serve
over spaghetti.

Serves 2.

UNCLE AL'S MEATBALLS

1½ lbs. ground beef
1 lb. ground pork
4 eggs
¼ cup milk
1 cup bread crumbs
¼ tsp. minced garlic
Salt & pepper
Oil
8-10 cups Spicy Tomato Sauce, page 96

Combine all ingredients except Spicy Tomato Sauce, and mix well. Roll into 1-inch balls. Brown well in oil. Drain, then add to Spicy Tomato Sauce, and simmer until meat is well cooked.

Serve over spaghetti.

Serves 8.

— Mary Alekson
Mississauga, Ontario

CHICKEN & SAUSAGE SPAGHETTI SAUCE

3 Tbsp. olive oil
4 cloves garlic, peeled & crushed
2 medium onions, chopped
1 lb. hot Italian sausage, cut into ½-inch slices
3 stalks celery, chopped
1 green pepper, chopped
6 leaves basil
1-2 tsp. oregano
Salt & pepper
Bay leaf
½ lb. mushrooms, sliced
28-oz. can tomatoes
13-oz. can tomato paste
1 chicken, boiled, boned & chopped
Parmesan cheese

Heat oil, and sauté garlic and onions until onions are limp. Add sausage and cook, stirring occasionally, until browned. Stir in celery, green pepper, basil, oregano, salt and pepper and bay leaf. Cook for 5 to 10 minutes. Add mushrooms and cook for 5 more minutes. Add tomatoes, tomato paste and chicken, and mix well.

Lower heat to simmer, cover, and cook for at least 1 hour, adding water if sauce becomes too thick. Serve over cooked pasta and top with Parmesan cheese.

Serves 8 to 10.

SPINACH & EGG NOODLES
WITH PEPPERS & SAUSAGE

THIS TASTY BLEND OF COMPLEMENTARY TEXTURES HAS PROVEN successful with either mild or hot Italian sausage.

3 large sweet red peppers
½ lb. Italian sausage, cut into ½-inch pieces
¼ cup water
¼ cup olive oil
3 Tbsp. finely chopped onion
3 tomatoes, coarsely chopped
¼ tsp. salt
Pepper
2 cups raw egg noodles
2 cups raw spinach noodles
2 Tbsp. butter
¾ cup Parmesan cheese

Cut peppers into 1-inch pieces. Cook sausage in water until liquid evaporates and meat is browned. Set aside. Drain fat from frying pan, add oil, and sauté onion until soft. Add tomatoes, salt, pepper and red peppers. Simmer, stirring, until peppers are soft − 6 to 7 minutes.

While sauce simmers, cook noodles. Drain, and place on a warmed platter. Pour sauce over noodles. Add butter, toss, add half the Parmesan cheese, toss again, and top with remaining cheese.

Serves 6.

— Holly Andrews
Puslinch, Ontario

GREEN PEPPER STEAK OVER NOODLES

2 lbs. round steak
2 onions, sliced
2 Tbsp. soya sauce
1 tsp. salt
⅛ tsp. pepper
2 cups beef stock
2 large green peppers, sliced
½ lb. mushrooms, sliced
3 Tbsp. cornstarch
6 cups cooked, buttered broad egg noodles

Slice beef diagonally into long, thin pieces. Brown in a heavy pot over low heat. Add onions, soya sauce, salt and pepper. Add beef stock, and simmer for 10 minutes. Add green peppers and mushrooms, and simmer for 10 minutes more.

Mix a few tablespoons of the hot sauce with the cornstarch, then stir back into pot. Cook until thickened. Serve over noodles.

Serves 4 to 6.

— Nora Scott
Millgrove, Ontario

ROTINI & SAUCE

¾ lb. rotini
¾ lb. ground beef
⅔ cup sliced carrots
⅔ cup sliced celery
⅔ cup sliced onion
Olive oil
1½ cups Spicy Tomato Sauce, page 96
Salt & pepper
1 tsp. oregano
Cayenne
1 clove garlic, minced
Parmesan cheese

Cook rotini in boiling, salted water for about 20 minutes, until tender.

Meanwhile, brown beef in a skillet, draining off excess fat.

Sauté carrots, celery and onion in oil over low heat for 5 minutes. Add Spicy Tomato Sauce, seasonings and cooked beef. Simmer, covered, for 10 minutes.

Drain and rinse rotini, and top with sauce and Parmesan cheese.

Serves 4.

— Glenn F. McMichael
Goderich, Ontario

FRIED NOODLES WITH BEEF & SNOW PEAS

16 oz. fine egg noodles
¾ cup oil
2 lbs. round steak, cut into thin strips
1 medium onion, sliced
2 cups beef stock
1 cup chopped mushrooms
2 Tbsp. dry sherry
2 Tbsp. soya sauce
3 Tbsp. cornstarch
8 oz. snow peas

Cook noodles in boiling, salted water until tender. Drain, rinse, and drain again. Heat ½ cup oil in heavy skillet. Add noodles and cook, turning occasionally, until browned — about 20 minutes.

Meanwhile, in another skillet, heat remaining ¼ cup oil. When hot, cook steak and onion until meat is browned, stirring constantly. Add stock, mushrooms, sherry and soya sauce. Combine cornstarch with ½ cup cold water, and gradually stir into skillet mixture. Cook, stirring, until thickened. Add snow peas and cook until heated through. Serve over noodles.

Serves 6.

SZECHUAN NOODLES

1 lb. spaghetti or Chinese noodles
2 Tbsp. oil
4 green onions, chopped
½ cup minced cooked ham
¼ cup chopped peanuts
⅓ cup sesame seeds
⅓ cup soya sauce
1 Tbsp. cider vinegar
1 tsp. honey
Tabasco sauce
2 Tbsp. catsup
⅔ cup chopped cucumber or celery

Cook noodles, drain, and toss with 1 Tbsp. oil. Set aside.

Stir-fry green onions in remaining oil for 1 minute. Add ham, peanuts, sesame seeds, soya sauce, vinegar, honey, Tabasco and catsup. Simmer 2 to 3 minutes, add cucumber or celery, and cook for a few minutes longer.

Add noodles, toss, and heat through.

— Bryanna Clark
Union Bay, British Columbia

PORK MEATBALLS & SPAGHETTI SAUCE

A VARIATION OF THE TRADITIONAL BEEF MEATBALLS, PORK MEATBALLS provide a flavourful addition to this spaghetti sauce, which is also enhanced by zucchini.

Meatballs
1 lb. ground pork
¼ cup Parmesan cheese
¼ cup oatmeal
½ cup chopped onion
3 Tbsp. chopped parsley
1 tsp. oregano
½ tsp. salt
¼ tsp. pepper
2 drops Tabasco sauce
1 Tbsp. oil

Sauce
28-oz. can tomatoes
6-oz. can tomato paste
¾ cup chopped celery
½ cup chopped green pepper
½ cup chopped green olives
1 tsp. oregano
1 tsp. basil
2 drops Tabasco sauce
¾ cup grated zucchini
1 cup chopped mushrooms

To make meatballs, combine pork, cheese, oatmeal, onion, parsley, oregano, salt, pepper and Tabasco sauce. Mix well and form into small balls. Refrigerate for 1 hour to allow to set. Heat oil in skillet, and brown meatballs on all sides. Drain on paper towels.

For sauce, combine tomatoes and tomato paste in large saucepan. Stir in celery, green pepper, olives, oregano, basil and Tabasco sauce. Bring to a boil, then drop in meatballs, zucchini and mushrooms. Simmer for 10 minutes, and serve over cooked spaghetti.

Serves 6 to 8.

STIR-FRIED GINGER BEEF
WITH BUTTERED PASTA

1½ lbs. lean beef, cut into thin strips
2 Tbsp. chopped ginger
4 cloves garlic, peeled & sliced
1 Tbsp. soya sauce
3 Tbsp. sesame oil
2 lbs. vermicelli
2 Tbsp. vegetable oil
1 Tbsp. cornstarch
4 carrots, thinly sliced
1 head broccoli, cut into small florets
½ lb. mushrooms, sliced
1 small zucchini, sliced
4 green onions, sliced
1 red pepper, sliced
½ lb. snow peas, broken into 1-inch pieces
Salt & pepper

Place beef, ginger and garlic in small bowl. Combine soya sauce and sesame oil, and mix with beef. Cover and let sit at room temperature for 30 minutes.

Cook pasta, drain, butter, and keep warm. Heat oil in wok. Combine cornstarch with 4 Tbsp. water, mix well, and stir into beef marinade. Pour into wok and stir-fry for 1 minute. Add carrots and broccoli and cook for 2 minutes. Add remaining vegetables, and stir-fry for 1 more minute, seasoning with salt and pepper to taste. Pour over pasta and serve.

Serves 8.

— Irene Louden
Port Coquitlam, British Columbia

DESSERTS

Desserts, like postscripts, contain the most succulent morsels

CANNOLI

A VARIATION OF THE BASIC PASTA RECIPE WHICH IS DEEP-FRIED AND THEN filled with sweetened ricotta cheese, cannoli originated in Sicily at the time of the Arab invasion. The cannoli are formed by wrapping the dough around a cannoli tube, a hollow metal tube which can be purchased at a kitchen supply store.

Cannoli
2 cups flour
2 Tbsp. lard
1 Tbsp. sugar
½ cup Marsala
1 egg, lightly beaten
4 cups oil

Filling
2 lbs. ricotta cheese
¾ cup icing sugar
6 Tbsp. chopped semisweet chocolate
Grated chocolate
Icing sugar

Place flour on working surface. Make a well in the centre, and add lard and sugar. Add Marsala gradually, incorporating enough to make a dough that will form a soft ball. Knead for about 10 minutes, or until it is glossy. Cover and set aside for 1 hour.

Cut dough in half. Roll as thin as possible by hand or by using a pasta machine. Cut into 4-inch circles. Wrap each circle around a cannoli tube. Overlap edges and seal with beaten egg. Repeat until all tubes are used up.

Heat oil to 375 degrees F. Cook tubes 2 at a time for about 1 minute, or until golden brown. Drain. After 10 seconds, carefully (they will be very hot) pull tube out of centre of cannoli. Repeat procedure until all dough has been used up.

For filling, mix together ricotta cheese, sugar and chocolate. When ready to serve, pipe filling into cannoli shells. Decorate with grated chocolate, and sprinkle with icing sugar.

FIOCCHI

THIS IS A DEEP-FRIED PASTA SHAPED LIKE BOW TIES AND THEN SPRINKLED with icing sugar.

6 Tbsp. sugar
1 tsp. lemon zest
1 tsp. orange zest
1 tsp. baking powder
2 cups flour
1 egg
½ cup melted butter
4 cups oil
Icing sugar

Combine sugar, lemon and orange zests, baking powder and 1¾ cups flour. Combine egg and butter, and add to dry ingredients, mixing well by hand or by blending in food processor to form a ball. If dough is too sticky, add more flour.

Roll out dough to ⅛-inch thickness, or put through pasta machine to third setting. Cut into 1½" x 4" rectangles. Cut a longitudinal 1-inch slit in the middle of each strip, put one end of rectangle through slit and pull flat.

Heat oil to 375 degrees F, and cook bow knots three or four at a time. Drain well, then sprinkle with icing sugar and serve.

Makes 12 bow knots.

— Mirella Guidi
Kingston, Ontario

NOODLES WITH POPPY SEEDS

A QUICK AND EASY DESSERT, THIS DISH CAN BE ENHANCED BY THE addition of chopped dried fruits or nuts.

½ cup milk
½ cup honey
1½ cups whipping cream
¼ cup ground poppy seeds
1 lb. egg noodles

Combine milk, honey, ½ cup whipping cream and poppy seeds in a small, heavy saucepan. Cook over medium-low heat for 5 to 8 minutes.

Meanwhile, cook the noodles until tender. Drain, and place in warmed, buttered serving dish. Pour sauce over noodles, toss well, and serve immediately, topped with the remaining 1 cup cream, whipped.

Serves 6 to 8.

— Nicky Webb
Bridesville, British Columbia

PASTA CANDY

8 oz. fusilli
Oil
1⅓ cups sugar
1 cup butter
½ cup light corn syrup
½ cup chopped pecans or walnuts
1 tsp. vanilla

Break fusilli into 2-inch pieces, and cook until tender. Drain and pat dry. Fry, 12 pieces at a time, in deep oil heated to 375 degrees F for 1 to 2 minutes, stirring to separate. Drain on paper towels, then place in greased 9" x 13" baking pan.

Combine sugar, butter and corn syrup. Cook, stirring, over medium heat until sugar dissolves and mixture comes to a boil. Cook, stirring occasionally, until candy thermometer reads 290 degrees F and syrup is golden. Remove from heat and stir in nuts and vanilla.

Quickly pour over fusilli, mix well and turn out. Break into pieces and store in airtight container.

Makes 16 cups.

— Christine Taylor
Norbertville, Quebec

NOODLE & PRUNE CASSEROLE

THIS DISH CAN BE SERVED TO ACCOMPANY A MAIN COURSE, BUT ALSO provides a delicious dessert, especially if topped with sweetened whipped cream.

½ lb. broad egg noodles
2 cups stewed, pitted prunes
½ cup chopped almonds
¼ cup butter
1 cup prune juice
1 tsp. cinnamon

Cook noodles until tender, then drain. Place alternate layers of noodles and prunes in a greased casserole dish, starting and ending with noodles and sprinkling almonds in the middle.

Melt butter in prune juice, and add cinnamon. If prunes are not sweet enough, add a bit of honey at this point.

Pour over casserole, and dot the top with a little butter. Bake at 350 degrees F for 20 minutes, or until the top begins to brown.

Serves 4.

— Mikell Billoki
Gore Bay, Ontario

SAUCY FRUITED LINGUINE

Orange Linguine
1½ cups flour
¼ tsp. shredded orange peel
1 egg, beaten
3 oz. orange juice concentrate, thawed
½ tsp. oil

Sauce
2 Tbsp. cornstarch
1 Tbsp. sugar
2 cups apricot nectar
½ stick cinnamon
2 cloves
3 cups peeled & sliced kiwis, peaches, apples, raspberries or strawberries
¼ cup white wine

To make linguine, combine flour and orange peel. Combine egg, juice and oil, and add to flour, mixing well.

Turn dough out onto lightly floured board, and knead until smooth. Cover and let rest for 10 minutes. Roll out or put through pasta machine until 1/16-inch thick. Cut into linguine.

For sauce, stir together cornstarch and sugar in large, heavy pot. Stir in apricot nectar, cinnamon and cloves. Cook, stirring, until bubbly. Reduce heat, cover, and simmer for 10 minutes, stirring occasionally. Strain and discard spices. Stir in fruit and wine and keep warm.

Cook linguine until tender, drain. Top with fruit sauce and serve.

Serves 8.

— Christine Taylor
Norbertville, Quebec

CARAMELIZED PASTA

3 cups flour
1½ tsp. baking powder
4 eggs
4 cups oil
3 cups sugar
½ tsp. white wine vinegar
4 Tbsp. sesame seeds

Combine flour, baking powder and eggs, mix well, and knead until smooth. Let rest, covered, for 15 minutes. Roll dough by hand to 1/16-inch thickness, or put through pasta machine to thinnest setting. Cut strips into 2-inch lengths, then cut, either by machine or by hand, into fettuccine-width noodles.

Heat oil to 375 degrees F, then fry noodles, a handful at a time, for 2 to 3 minutes, or until puffed and golden. Drain, and place in a large bowl.

Heat sugar and vinegar in heavy pot until sugar is dissolved, stirring constantly. Cook, without stirring, until syrup is light caramel.

Pour over noodles, add sesame seeds, and toss to coat. Place in greased 9" x 13" pan, press to form a smooth top, and let cool.

Makes 16 pieces.

KUGEL

A TRADITIONAL SABBATH DISH, KUGEL IS ALSO PREPARED FOR OTHER Jewish holidays and family meals. It may be varied with such simple additions as tofu, yogurt, chopped apple or other fruit.

½ lb. wide noodles
3 Tbsp. melted butter
3 eggs, separated
¼ cup raisins
¼ cup chopped almonds
½ cup crushed pineapple
1 tsp. cinnamon
¼ cup honey (optional)

Cook noodles in boiling, salted water until tender, and drain. Add butter, beaten egg yolks, raisins, almonds, pineapple and cinnamon. Add honey if kugel is to be served as a dessert.

Beat egg whites until stiff and fold into pudding. Mix well, and pour into a well-greased casserole. Bake at 350 degrees F for 45 minutes, or until browned.

Serves 4 to 6.

— Mikell Billoki
Gore Bay, Ontario

NOODLE PUDDING WITH LEMON SAUCE

Pudding
2 Tbsp. butter
8 oz. broad egg noodles, cooked & drained
3 eggs, separated
½ cup honey
1½ tsp. cinnamon
2 apples, sliced
¼ cup currants
½ cup chopped nuts

Sauce
½ cup honey
2 Tbsp. cornstarch
2 cups boiling water
Rind & juice of 1 lemon
2 Tbsp. butter

Heat butter in skillet, add noodles, and cook just long enough to absorb butter. Remove from heat. Beat egg yolks and add to noodles along with honey, cinnamon, apples, currants and nuts. Beat egg whites until stiff and add to pudding. Place in greased baking dish and bake at 350 degrees F for 30 minutes.

Meanwhile, prepare sauce. Combine honey and cornstarch in saucepan. Add boiling water slowly, stirring constantly. Cook for 10 minutes, then add lemon rind and juice and butter. Serve with pudding.

Serves 8 to 10.

— Nicky Webb
Bridesville, British Columbia

INDEX